The Source for Developmental Coordination Disorder

Paulene H. Kamps

Skill Area:	Developmental Coordination Disorder
Ages:	3 through 18
Grades:	PreK through 12

LinguiSystems, Inc.
3100 4th Avenue
East Moline, IL 61244-9700
800-776-4332
FAX: 800-577-4555
E-mail: service@linguisystems.com
Web: linguisystems.com

Printed in the U.S.A.

ISBN 0-7606-0613-7

Paulene Kamps

■ **Paulene H. Kamps**, Ph.D., is a kinesiologist, educator, and chartered psychologist who works with children, teenagers, and young adults with various learning problems and disabilities. She has worked as a teacher, play therapist, learning strategist, and educational psychologist at various agencies and for different school boards in Alberta, Canada. She also has a private practice in the area of psychology. Paulene has worked with people who have Down syndrome, various developmental delays, Asperger syndrome; all types of learning disabilities, attention deficit, gross motor coordination difficulties; and other cognitive, emotional, behavioral, and/or physical problems. Paulene consults with parents and professionals in the fields of medicine and education as well as school boards. She conducts assessments, provides strategies and direct support for students with learning problems, and she leads various workshops and training sessions. She was educated in many different disciplines at the University of Calgary and thoroughly enjoys her chosen career path.

Because she is a mother and was a classroom teacher for many years, Paulene brings compassion and unique clinical skills to her profession. She and her husband, Don, parent four healthy and active children – the oldest of whom provided artwork for this resource.

The Source for Developmental Coordination Disorder is Paulene's first publication with LinguiSystems.

Edited by Carolyn LoGiudice
Page Layout by Lisa Parker
Cover Design by Jason Platt

Acknowledgments

■ Many thanks to the people who were directly involved in the publication of this book. Marion Prins helped organize and compile the references. Carolyn LoGiudice worked tirelessly to edit and organize the manuscript. Thanks to Lisa Parker for her efforts in layout and design and to Margaret Warner, who provided additional visual graphics. I also wish to acknowledge the help and support of my current and previous colleagues as well as any other people who worked "behind the scenes" to make this project a reality. Thanks to you all!

■ This book was illustrated by **Joal J. Kamps** and **Margaret Warner**.

Joal, the author's oldest son, is a musician, a poet, and a visual artist who has worked at many interesting jobs to date: coffee barista, painter, horse care attendant at a riding stable, employee at a sign/print shop, and international model.

Margaret attended St. Ambrose University in Davenport, Iowa, where she studied art. She has worked as an artist for over 22 years and began illustrating materials for LinguiSystems in 1988. Since then, Margaret has illustrated more than 100 books, cards, stickers, and games for LinguiSystems.

Dedications

■ **To the parents/caregivers of children with motor coordination problems**
You dared enough to share your stories and pain with me; you showed a willingness to read, listen, watch, and learn; and then, by encouraging your child to participate in the various programs I have offered, you courageously allowed someone you didn't know very well to try new educational approaches with your precious sons and daughters. I'm proud to have been given the opportunity to meet and work with you and your children. It was an incredible experience to help and observe your sons and daughters learn and practice so many new skills on their own. Thank you for your trust. Even though I was already convinced I had the best job in the world, you actually paid me to play with and teach your children. It doesn't get much better than that!

With Gratitude

With Gratitude

◼ **To the many teachers and other professionals who, after seeing and hearing about my work at local conferences and workshops, referred their students and clients with motor learning difficulties to me**

You also took a large step of faith to recommend families into my care. You must have felt that I had something valuable and interesting to offer to the children you referred, and I am very grateful for your confidence in my skill set and techniques. You encouraged me to share this information with a much larger audience by writing a book. I did and here it is! I hope other professionals like you will also learn and consider using these techniques to address similar issues with the many children we all work with.

◼ **To my husband, Don, and our four children: Joal, Jessiya, Sanchia, and Jonah**

Thanks for your patience. This writing project took much longer than I thought, and you had to give much to the running of our family. Let this dedication be one small way I can give back to you.

◼ **To my God**

The more I read, study, listen, and watch, the more I understand the little I really know about the wonder of this world and everything in and around it. It is an incredible masterpiece. Even the wisest man who ever lived was unable to comprehend how all things fit together (Ecclesiastes 1:1-12:14).

I believe God simply wants us to do the best we can with the skills, abilities, knowledge, and gifts He has given to us. This book sprang from a desire to please Him and to help people who have difficulties in learning and developing in the psychomotor domain.

I want to publicly thank my God for "opening doors" and providing many opportunities to accomplish all the certificates, degrees, and experience to be considered knowledgeable in this field. I know with certainty that this is my area of passion and sense that this is what I have been "called" to do. I am humbled by that honor. I also consider it a real privilege and joy to be able to share some of my knowledge with you now.

Table of Contents

Whats Inside

"A-ha" Experience

Children who struggle with motor coordination and have difficulty acquiring fundamental motor skills have intrigued me for many years. I recall noticing at a very young age that some of my classmates stood beside the wall of the school during recess and lunchtime, or they wandered to the edge of the playground, stood by the fence, and from that distance watched other classmates play.

Although I was neither exceptionally gifted in sports nor the weakest athlete in school, I remember being one of the last three or four students picked for teams in physical education. I also recall being thankful that I was not one of the last two students who teachers eventually assigned to the various teams. Those are the students I have wondered about for many years. Maybe with that thought buried unconsciously, I have spent many years gaining the required education, skill set, and training to work with this group. Then years ago, I had an "a-ha" experience.

To satisfy my own general curiosity and to stay abreast of research findings in my areas of interest (education, kinesiology, and psychology), I read many articles about the effect of motor problems on psychosocial development. Then I went to an evening presentation on this topic. After about 15 to 20 minutes, I thought, "These kids have a name! Wow! There is even a diagnostic term for what these kids have – *Developmental Coordination Disorder*!" That incident prompted an incredible thirst for knowledge in this area. And so the birth of this book began.

Message to the Reader

I am very pleased that you have taken the time to pick up this book. I hope you will find the material interesting, easy to read, and full of valuable information.

◼ Purpose

There are five main goals for this book:

1 To help people understand how gross motor skills typically develop

2 To describe the main factors and conditions that may cause children to have problems with learning and performing motor skills. There is also an explanation of what types of behaviors you may see if a child has motor difficulties. Furthermore, there is an explanation of how motor problems can impact the child's functioning in other domains of behavior.

3 To highlight what is currently known about developmental coordination disorder (DCD). You will also come to know a bit about some other conditions or disorders that impact motor learning and performance.

4 To offer many common-sense strategies to assist children who have difficulties coordinating physical movement

5 To provide a comprehensive list of references on this topic. This list will show you that the study of and intervention with children with DCD is a very credible topic, researched all over the world and studied by numerous people with a wide range of skills, abilities, and training. There will be many references you can peruse to read and learn more about this subject if you so desire.

◼ Writing Style

I am especially happy to write this book for parents, educators, coaches, therapists, doctors, and any others who play and work or are in any way directly involved with children with motor problems. I am also relieved that I can finally write using my natural writing style. During my studies at the graduate level, I learned very quickly that the way I documented my ideas on paper did not fit the expectations of numerous professors. Academic writing did not come naturally for me. I experienced "writer's block" several times as I struggled for months, trying to rewrite several chapters of my dis- sertation in such a way that it would meet the needs of the instructional staff

Message to the Reader

at the university I attended. I heard many times that my writing was very easy to read, but that it was too casual. I even recall having a conversation with one professor during which time I said, "But I *want* parents and others to read my work. I want the information to make sense to them. *They* are the ones who are working with their children on a daily basis." Now that the academic standards have been attained and I have many years of experience to draw on, I can finally write information in an easy-to-read manner that will, hopefully, make sense to those who want to learn about this topic.

The information presented in this resource comes directly from diverse academic references, scientific articles, and research studies, many of which are challenging to read. I have tried to integrate this information in a more reader-friendly style without inserting all the references throughout the body of the book. For those of you who are interested in reading the academic articles and papers, references are included at the end of each chapter, and, as mentioned previously, there is a more comprehensive reference list at the back of the book (pp. 163-187), which you are welcome to investigate on your own.

In addition to the material supplied by academic journals and articles, much of what you will read is the result of some personal creative moments, daily interactions with my four children and their friends, an artistic son, a very supportive family, friends who talk with me about my work, my own efforts with children with motor coordination difficulties, and the advice and suggestions provided by parents who have a son or daughter with motor problems. I hope that the blend of knowledge acquired through the research literature and the day-to-day interactions with parents and children with motor difficulties will make this a very practical resource.

For Professionals

If you are like me, there are certain books or manuals that you keep pulling off the shelf in your office because you like the way the information is presented. The content is written in a manner that is easy to paraphrase to others, and the intervention ideas actually make sense and are doable with a minimum amount of cost and extra energy. These precious resources soon become dog-eared from being carried in briefcases, marked up with sticky notes, and even lent to others. I hope this book becomes one of those prized possessions.

With your skills, training, and professional experience, you may already know much of what you will read in this book. If so, this resource provides a quick refresher of what you have learned over the years. You will see that the information is presented in a way that will address a wide audience. Consider this book a supplemental resource for yourself and/or offer it to parents in addition to your personal and professional skills.

I also understand that you may be aware of specific research studies or journal articles that oppose some of the information in this book. I have chosen to present general statements rather than specific, single-study findings because this is an enormous topic; it is far too complex and difficult to document every related topic that has been studied over the last 40 years. I have read and followed the research trends very closely for many years and have summarized them in general statements in this book.

Finally, I hope you recognize the value in providing basic knowledge and practical tips to many nonprofessionals using an informal style for general readability. After all, when the professionals have completed their assessments, diagnosis, therapies, programs, and specialized interventions, it will be parents and other caregivers who may or may not choose to follow-up with the additional time, energy, and effort needed to support and encourage their sons and daughters. Therefore, let us, in whatever way possible, encourage parents, teachers, therapists, and other service providers to learn all they can. If what is presented here helps even one child learn to ride a bicycle, throw a ball properly, or join peers at play, then writing this book was worth it and my goal has been accomplished.

■ For Parents

Parents, if you have a child with motor problems who seems to fit the criteria for developmental coordination disorder (DCD) as described in this book, you may be surprised to learn that there really is an identifiable diagnosis for your child's condition! You will need to find a professional who knows.

The news that there really is a reason for your child's motor difficulties may provide a bit of relief initially, since you've always known something was "different" about your child, and now you have that confirmation. You can even share your newfound knowledge with others. However, you may also be particularly pained by some of the information you read here. For example, there is currently no known cure for specific conditions that impact gross

Message to the Reader

and/or fine motor skill learning and performance. Rather, interventions help but do not actually cure the underlying problem. Unfortunately, scientific studies indicate that the traditional bottom-up forms of treatment (e.g., sensory integration, process-oriented treatment, perceptual motor training, and similar combinations as described in the literature) do not offer long-term, sustained gains in functioning. Most current research findings are not highly supportive of such programs, for many studies have shown that interventions given by highly qualified professionals (e.g., occupational and/or physical therapists) based primarily on these treatment models do not facilitate the transfer or generalization of specifically learned skills to other motor activities. That does not mean, however, that none of their intervention methods work.

Most occupational and physical therapists (OTs and PTs) are excellent clinicians who use an eclectic or multifaceted approach to treatment that encompasses many different theories and methods. These therapists usually obtain positive results because they don't quit until they see improvements of some type. It is just that research shows that "pure" types of bottom-up treatment formats are not successful in the long-term as was once thought. Nevertheless, these comments do not suggest that you should not use the services of an occupational or physical therapist. They are very skilled professionals who have a great deal of wisdom and skill to offer to you and your children. Just request information about their treatment modality and ask for stories of their successes with children. What are the students able to do now that they were unable to do several months ago? Are the gains sustained?

Furthermore, a skilled OT or PT may be a very important resource for you. These professionals generally have the assessment tools and skill sets needed to recognize whether a child's motor difficulties are delayed or simply different. In addition, they have been trained to determine whether the child's motor difficulties are related to muscle tone, range of motion, strength, musculo-skeletal problems or deformities, and/or other such conditions. In addition, they can assess balance skills, fine motor dexterity, gross motor coordination, sensory integration problems, and/or motor planning problems. Therefore, they can do part of the assessment required before you visit a specialist about your son or daughter's motor concerns. In essence, if they have tested your child and found significant motor delays that are not due to any physical problem, then this information can be reported to your medical specialist. Your OT's or PT's report should actually expedite the doctor's decision to consider DCD as a possibility. If the doctor determines, for example, that your child's motor difficulties are also not due to a neurological impairment (or other childhood condition, as discussed in Chapter Three, pp. 93-101), then DCD may be the resultant diagnosis.

Message to the Reader

There is hope! Other forms of treatment are beginning to reveal results. As mentioned earlier, the goals of this book are to "tell it like it is" and then offer some new suggestions for how to work with children with motor problems by suggesting interventions that utilize a "top-down" approach. The suggestions presented in this book are gaining credibility since they are based on research conducted in the last ten to fifteen years. Findings show positive results in the acquisition of motor skills and coordination after using a metacognitive approach. Of course you do not need to accept this as the only strategy to use with your child; it is simply presented for your information and consideration. I invite you to try this option because the students and parents I have worked with are thrilled with the results.

■ Content Overview

If you are like me, most of you will now want to flip to the final section of the book right away. Instead, try to read the book from front to back because it was prepared in a manner that will encourage one topic to flow to another logically.

*   First you will learn the basic principles associated with motor skill development.

*   Next you will read what may be hindering your child's learning of gross motor skills. After an extensive list of the types of problems you may witness in children with motor coordination problems, there is a detailed description of developmental coordination disorder (DCD) and brief summaries of other conditions with motor-related problems.

*   This information is followed by a short introduction and other background information about the metacognitive approach to intervention. I hope this information will help you understand why this method offers hope for the person with motor difficulties.

*   By reading and using the different ideas supplied in the last part of the book, you can then apply the metacognitive approach when working with your student, son, daughter, or client.

*   At the end of this book, there is an extensive list of references on DCD and motor learning, which rounds out the resource.

Message to the Reader

■ Gender Issues

I wish to clarify the way gender issues will be addressed within this book. Although research has shown that it is more common for boys to have coordination problems than girls, gender references in this book will be alternated. Also, because I hope that many parents, teachers, therapists, and other professionals will purchase this book as a resource, I acknowledge that the individuals they work with are also identified as *students*, *clients*, and *patients*.

As you read this resource, you will find that, for the most part, I refer to the child with motor problems as *your child*, as from a parent's or caregiver's perspective. That does not mean I am ignoring other relationships with professional adults. Actually, the term *your child* is used purposefully as an inclusive statement since it is not uncommon for teachers to comment *my student* and for doctors and other medical staff to use terms such as *my patient* or *my client*. Therefore, *your child* in this book indicates any person under the age of 18 years.

■ Feedback

I would appreciate feedback on this book. If you have found it useful or have discovered some other strategies that work for your son/daughter, student, or client, I would love to hear from you. If you find some areas in this resource that could use a more detailed explanation, please contact me as well. Although I cannot promise to write each of you a personal note back, I will greatly appreciate your input or critique.

Paulene Kamps

Contact Information: **drkamps@telusplanet.net**

Our Stories

66 I just don't understand it! Even though we have put Joshua into organized sports from infancy onwards – in swimming, gymnastics, and soccer, for example – he still looks and acts like it's his first time in any program. He has a horrible time learning motor skills. His printing is absolutely terrible and he still can't cut his own meat or tie his shoelaces. He gets petrified when we ask him about learning to ride a scooter.

I guess we should be happy with the little things. Like, he just had his eighth birthday and now is able to cut his own waffles! 99

◆ ◆ ◆

66 Can you believe that there are kids out there who don't like physical education? I can't either, but let me tell you about one in my class. Svetlanna does not participate in activities during my PE class. She is scared of balls and always seems to have some excuse about why she can't join in. It is very normal for her to go stand or sit against the wall in the gym. I am not sure how to engage her in activities anymore. No students ever choose her or ask her to join their teams, and I have never seen her smile in this class.

When I insist that Svetlanna participate, she runs around the gym looking goofy and reckless, and she doesn't seem to have a clue about how to hold the various pieces of sports equipment or what to do with them. I'm not sure whether it is the result of lack of experience with the different types of sporting equipment or she simply doesn't want to do the different activities. I find that very hard to differentiate. She seems smart enough, though, and she listens attentively when I give instructions. It's weird. It's like she *can't* do what is required in class. 99

◆ ◆ ◆

66 My son, Lukas, has delays in many motor areas. He was slow to learn to stand and walk, and his speech was also very slow to develop. We heard from a speech-language therapist that it is quite common for children with motor difficulties to have problems when they are learning to talk because speech is an oral-motor control skill. I never knew that. As time went on, Lukas did learn to run, but he still hasn't mastered jumping with both feet at the same time, and he can't yet throw or catch a ball properly. I know these are not critical life skills, but there were a few motor skills that we had a very hard time teaching him.

I feel a little embarrassed telling you this, but he was almost seven when he was fully toilet trained. He had a very difficult time learning to wipe his bottom. This is a very important life skill! Once again, we heard from another specialist that going to the bathroom may be more difficult for a child with motor delays. That is because bowel and bladder control are also motor activities that both require sequential muscle action. I never knew that before either.

Our Stories

Anyway, now that Lukas has learned to stay dry at night and manipulate toilet paper properly, he is able to go to his grandparents' house for an overnight visit. Thankfully, they invite him regularly. None of his classmates invite him to anything or anywhere. Oh, well, my husband and I are truly thankful that Lukas has accomplished these two bathroom feats! **"**

◆ ◆ ◆

" Something doesn't quite make sense to me. My daughter, Elsa, can do some motor activities just fine, but she can't do other things. As a matter of fact, her motor development has always been very puzzling to me because it has been so inconsistent. For example, Elsa can play with Legos building blocks for hours and create remarkable objects, and she can hit a baseball just fine. She loves splashing around in the swimming pool, but even though she thinks she is good at swimming, she finds it very difficult to coordinate her arms and legs when doing the front crawl. She cannot run and is not agile enough to climb, yet she learned to ride a bicycle with no problem! Elsa also finds it very difficult to write or draw. I've also discovered that she prefers to wear jogging pants and T-shirts because they are easier to slip on than dresses with zippers or blouses with small buttons or tight-fitting jeans. I sure wonder what is going on and how I can help her. **"**

◆ ◆ ◆

" I feel bad about all the times I have watched Mohammed on the baseball field and talked to him later about not putting forth acceptable effort. It is very hard to watch him because it looks like he is not trying very hard, but it is even harder to watch when it is apparent that he *is* putting forth his best effort and he cannot keep up.

As always, there are keen parents who like to comment and criticize, which is very hard to listen to. I am most concerned that other kids will begin to become less tolerant and that participation will become more and more difficult for Mohammed. He so badly wants to be there. **"**

◆ ◆ ◆

" Oh, my goodness! I have just come to realize something. When you first asked me if Maria-Rose could tie her shoes, cut her meat, pour her milk, and make sandwiches, I said she could. But I just now realized that I have been doing all that stuff for her for years! You know, I honestly don't know if she can do any of those things. It was when you asked about the sandwiches that I finally 'got it'. She doesn't make sandwiches. She always asks me to fix her something good to eat and, of course, I like to make her happy, so I do it. When I have too much to do and she's hungry, I have seen her take two pieces of bread, slap a piece of

Our Stories

luncheon meat between them, and start eating. I always thought she was starving and couldn't wait to eat, but, as you commented, maybe it's because she has trouble spreading butter, mayonnaise, and mustard. I had never even thought about that possibility.

And now I need to tell you that I don't know if she can fasten her shoes. She always just slips her shoes on. I always pour her milk and juice so she doesn't spill, and I also cut up her meat and prepare her food on the plate before I hand it to her. I have no idea what she can do. I have been doing all kinds of things for her the last few years. Why, I even put the toothpaste on her toothbrush and leave it on the bathroom sink for her! I thought I was saving her some time, and frankly, I'd rather do these little things than clean up behind her. Oh, my! I feel like a terrible mother! 99

◆ ◆ ◆

66 My older son, Owen, has had years of programming with various therapists. Nothing seems to help and no one seems to know what the problem is. He still can't tie his shoes or use a knife and fork properly, and his writing is absolutely awful. He says he is tired of going to therapy or any other type of program. I try to help in simple ways, like making sure that his shoes are the Velcro kind, preparing his lunches, and zipping up his jacket before he heads off to school in the morning. I've also started letting him spend more time playing computer games. I really don't like it when Owen sits in front of the computer screen so much, but he simply doesn't appear interested in the kinds of outdoor and physically active events that other boys his age are into. Marty, our other son, will simply pick up a hockey stick, head out the door, and start shooting pucks into the hockey net. Before you know it, three other neighborhood kids join him. But not Owen.

I guess I try to rationalize it by saying that I want to make sure Owen gets a feeling of success somewhere, and computer games give him that. He hates to join any school or community function where games and sports are played because he is always left out. If he does join in, others often laugh and make fun of him. And then, to top it off, if he joins a team and they happen to lose, the other kids will often blame him for their team's loss. I've even witnessed it. When that happens, I sometimes don't blame Owen for not wanting to join in.

Owen's difficulties seem to be affecting our whole family. We don't do things together – like ride bikes, play catch, or even go hiking as a family. Marty says that I am treating Owen like a baby by buying him Velcro shoes, and he gets mad when we don't let *him* sit in front of the computer as much as Owen.

Our Stories

What scares me most is that it seems like Owen is giving up trying to learn and that he is getting more and more angry. He is acting out more at school, and he already doesn't have many friends there. I am scared that this is going to escalate. We really don't know what to do about it. Frankly, my husband and I are tired of pouring money into programs that don't seem to make a difference anyway. **"**

◆ ◆ ◆

Some of these stories could have been written by you, while other quotes may be the types of thoughts you have had but never shared with anyone. For example, you may be very embarrassed about your child's poor motor skills because you love sports and similar recreational activities, and you so much want her to be able to do some of the basic skills that brought you pleasure as a child. You've heard many people refer to the benefits of getting children to be physically active during their formative years so they will remain active throughout their lives. You already know the importance of physical activity, and want to instill the concept of a healthy, active lifestyle in your child. You recognized years ago that your child had some trouble with motor skills, but you thought that giving her lots of opportunity to learn and practice would help her "get it" sooner or later. After the money you've sunk into community sports programs, Little League, gymnastics lessons, dance classes, and other such activities, you thought she would have caught the idea somehow – all to no avail. You have detected only very slight improvements, and now you have run out of ideas. You don't know what else to do.

◆ ◆ ◆

You may be a dad who has heard from your co-workers and other parents whose children excel in athletics that sports are "awesome." Sports help kids to gain confidence and self-esteem, to be included in peer groups, and to stay busy and out of trouble. You know that from personal experience, but your child is not good at sports and does not like anything related to physical activity. According to your "ex," your son is alone most of the time. Almost every time you call to talk to him, he's at home, perched in front of the TV or the computer.

Now that he is staying at your home for two weeks this summer, you are starting to worry about how he is going to fill his days and what you are going to do next month when you and Margaret are on vacation with him.

You used to play football in college and always dreamed of the day that you and your son would play catch in the park and you could teach him some of the basics of the game. You had even planned to coach for one of the teams he played on when he was a little older, but that was before the divorce. Your son is almost ten years old now and never wants to do anything physical with

Our Stories

you. He seems to be content to sit and watch TV most of the time. Oh, how you wish you could convince him to come outdoors to play catch with you, even for half an hour or so. The only two times he did, you noticed that he actually seemed scared of the ball. You remember how weird it seemed – he shut his eyes, turned his head, and put his hands in front of his face. Actually, if you really analyzed what was going on, he seemed to cower when you threw him a pass! Although you still want him to learn the basics of the game, and you'd even be willing to use one of those foam-type footballs, you are embarrassed to be seen throwing gentle underhand passes to your almost teenaged son. People driving by in their cars might think *you* have no idea how to throw a football properly! If they only knew.

❖ ❖ ❖

As Jakki's mother, you have shared your concerns with your doctor about your daughter's slow movements and delays in learning to run, bounce a ball, and ride a bicycle. The doctor already assured you several visits ago that Jakki does not have cerebral palsy or any other neurological condition, yet Jakki still seems to have trouble moving with any kind of consistency. She does not display motor control in many activities, and, if the truth be known, she looks very "different" when she moves. As a matter of fact, others have already noticed that she appears very awkward and uncoordinated at playtime. Although Jakki is able to read and do most of the activities required in her second-grade classroom, you know that something is wrong.

❖ ❖ ❖

Your situation may be different. Even though you yourself are not interested in athletics and sports, you have seen your son with other children and know that he is lacking basic motor skills such as running, jumping, kicking, catching, throwing, and most other activities that his peers participate in. You don't expect your child to be a champion athlete, but you earnestly hope that he will have some basic skills to use with peers and friends at school and in the neighborhood. You have tried and tried to help your son learn to ride a bicycle, skate, print neater, hit a baseball, etc., but all your efforts have been unsuccessful. You are giving up and think that because you can't teach him these types of activities, you might be lacking in some of your parenting skills. You are getting tired of trying to help your child and are very confused about what the problem is and, most of all, how to solve it. You want help but don't know whom to ask.

❖ ❖ ❖

Our Stories

Perhaps you head into the school one morning in hopes of finding Ms. Roberts, your daughter's fourth-grade teacher. You want to get her opinion about Becky's skills in school because you have noticed that Becky is not interested in playing outdoors when she is at home. She just sits and reads books and watches TV for most of the day.

When you finally find her and have a few moments to talk, Ms. Roberts confirms what you thought; Becky is not as skilled as her peers in the gym. The teacher goes on to explain that, based on the law of averages, not all children will be good in physical activities, so you shouldn't worry. Ms. Roberts comments that you should be thankful Becky is into the more academic skills, such as reading, listening to music, typing on the computer, and watching educational programs on TV, instead of playing physically active games. Becky's teacher compliments you on all the background knowledge Becky has as a result of her reading and television viewing.

Then Ms. Roberts tells you one more time that you shouldn't worry about the "sports stuff" anyway. Becky will be fine without it. As you prepare to leave, Ms. Roberts quickly adds that your concern may be better directed at improving Becky's printing and handwriting skills, since that is a more noticeable problem in school.

◆ ◆ ◆

A new teacher comments he has noticed that your child, Alexander, is unable to use scissors and cut paper properly, has messy coloring skills, and does not like to fold papers, paste, or perform other craft activities. This teacher encourages you to work with Alexander in the evenings and on the weekends. You have heard similar comments from Alexander's previous teachers, but none of them knows how much you have tried to help him. Furthermore, you have run out of ideas for ways to help Alexander. Nevertheless, you once again contain your emotions, even though you really want to yell out, "You're the educator! Why don't **you** figure out ways to help him, for goodness' sake?"

◆ ◆ ◆

18

Our Stories

The one and only time you explained your child's poor motor skills and the related concerns to your pediatrician, she replied, "Yes, some children are more clumsy than others at this age." However, the pediatrician quickly added, "There is nothing medically wrong with your child, so you shouldn't fret about it. She seems bright enough and such children generally grow out of it in time." Even though it's been a few years, you haven't dared to bring it up again, especially with her.

◆ ◆ ◆

For a long time now, you have sensed a widening gap between your child's abilities and the athletic skills of your nieces and nephews who are the same age. You have also noticed differences between your child and your friends' children. Even the younger neighbor kids can do a lot of things better than your child. What bothers you most, though, is that you've become aware that your child is purposely avoiding any physical or sports-related activity, especially if other children are nearby.

Like many of the people identified in the scenarios above, you may feel very discouraged and upset, and think you have nowhere else to turn. No one seems to understand what you are concerned about, and you have no idea whom or what to ask, even if you should happen to find someone with a listening ear. You feel very alone. And concerned. And confused. And frustrated.

This resource was written for you.

If any of the previous scenarios sound like your situation, then *The Source for Developmental Coordination Disorder* is the resource for you. It explains basic information about motor skill development, possible causes of motor difficulties, the kinds of activities your child may have trouble with, and strategies that may help your child overcome these problems. This book offers some information you may never have heard before. For example, you might be surprised that research shows that difficulties in the motor domain can eventually affect other domains of human functioning; motor difficulties can affect social relationships with peers.

If what you read in this book describes your son or daughter, or someone else you know or work with, it is important to have your child assessed properly by a qualified professional. Before you visit the specialist, though, read through this book to get some background knowledge about motor skills and how your concerns relate to this information.

Our Stories

As you read this resource and other information about motor difficulties, highlight or mark certain pages as needed. Then use the information to talk to your medical practitioner about your "gut feelings." Remember that, although the diagnostic criteria for developmental coordination disorder (DCD) and descriptions of several other conditions are included in this book, and you may feel that one better suits your child than another, it is still the doctor's or other specialist's training, skill set, and experience with numerous children over many years that will allow the professional to make the appropriate diagnosis. Also, do not be surprised if the doctor you see has not yet heard of DCD. It is almost impossible for busy professionals to stay current with the research literature, so, although DCD has been researched thoroughly for many years, very few practitioners are making this diagnosis in North America because they are simply unaware of this condition. If you think the DCD diagnosis applies to your son or daughter, consider taking this book along and showing your medical professional all the references in the back of the book. It will provide the credibility the doctor likely requires.

What is probably more important than your doctor having time to read all the literature on DCD and other motor coordination problems, is that your doctor come to understand how motor problems affect children negatively in many domains of behavior. That is why it is critical for motor-related conditions to be recognized and diagnosed!

I sincerely hope that this book will answer some questions you have had for years about your child. Often just finding out what is causing your child's difficulties is a valuable breakthrough. Even though you may have felt your concerns were exaggerated sometimes, now you will *know* you were right to wonder for years what was going on with your child.

Remember, though, finding out what is causing your child's motor problem is only part of the solution. The rest has to do with what can be done about it. That is where your role as a parent, a teacher, a therapist, or other caregiver comes in. You will need to be a strong advocate for your child's needs.

I sincerely hope that this resource will allow you to begin your journey of learning about DCD. Together, let's aim to read, listen, watch, and learn about this topic so we can give the children we work and live with the help and hope they deserve!

◆ ◆ ◆

This book is about developmental coordination disorder (DCD), a condition that impacts motor skill development. In order to determine if a student or young child has problems with developing and performing motor skills, which is the primary factor in children with DCD, one must have a solid understanding of the general principles involved in motor skill acquisition. To facilitate this understanding, this chapter presents an overview of two aspects of motor skill development:

1 the basic motor skill progression children typically pass through in their formative years

2 factors that impact the acquisition and/or proficiency and performance of motor skills

The information in this chapter comes from numerous sources. Data about motor skill development and movement assessment comes from researchers and clinicians in physical education, pediatrics/child development, occupational and physical therapy (OT and PT), psychology, and neuropsychology. These various disciplines have categorized the development of motor skills in many different ways. The following is a compilation of different research findings blended together. It is presented in hopes that you will understand the general principles of growth and development in the motor domain.

■ How Motor Skills Develop

One of the marvelous things about working with children with motor coordination difficulties is showing and explaining to parents, teachers, and other interested parties that motor skills tend to be established in an orderly pattern. Many parents have unknowingly witnessed these predictable stages, while numerous researchers have documented the wonderful developmental sequence of motor skill acquisition.

There is a wonderful developmental sequence for motor skill acquisition.

Although there are exceptions to the normal developmental sequence – and your child or the child you work with may be one of those exceptions – from birth until adolescence, a child generally passes through the progressions listed in the box on page 23 and discussed below. Keep in mind that many factors account for much of the individual variance among children developing motor skills. These include the following:

• the child's overall physical maturation

• genetic influences

• environmental circumstances, such as socio-economic conditions and opportunities

• cultural and ethnic factors

The influence of these factors on motor skill development will be further described on pages 26-36.

For various reasons, all children do not follow precisely the same pattern in developing motor skills.

1 Involuntary Actions → Voluntary Actions

An infant tends to display reflex actions (involuntary attempts to move) before exhibiting purposeful movements (voluntary activity). One of the first motions a baby makes is a strong sucking action. This reflex action is important for basic survival (acquiring the necessary food to live) and is also a foundation for later language development. As the infant comes to understand the rewards associated with the reflex activity (for example, locating food, feeling the warmth and comfort and enjoying the other sensations of the feeding/holding process), the infant will repeat the actions. Involuntary movements eventually become voluntary as the baby actively looks to repeat the pleasurable experience and sensations.

Chapter One

Sequence of Developing Motor Skills

1 **Involuntary Actions → Voluntary Actions**

2 **Cephalo Control → Caudal Control**

3 **Flexion → Extension**

4 **Proximal Control → Distal Control**

5 **Stationary Position → Locomotor Action**

6 **Undifferentiated Movement → Differentiated Movement**

7 **Gross Motor Control → Fine Motor Control**

8 **Simple Skills → Complex Skills**

9 **Control of the Body → Control of Objects**

10 **Large and Near → Small and Far**

11 **Stable Environment → Changing Environment**

Chapter One

2 **Cephalo Control → Caudal Control**

Children gain control of the head and neck (cephalo area) before they gain control of movements in the lower or "tail" (caudal) area of the body. This sequence also suggests that children gain rudimentary control of the mouth at an early age and before other limbs and parts of the body further away from the head.

> *Although there are some suggestions in this book for children with oral motor difficulties, there are many other excellent resources that provide more in-depth detail. For the purposes of this book, the emphasis is primarily on gross motor control and, to a lesser degree, fine motor control.*

3 **Flexion → Extension**

Infants are able to purposefully bend (flex) their arms, legs, and other joints, as when curling into a fetal position, before they can intentionally straighten (extend) their limbs, as when standing upright without support.

4 **Proximal Control → Distal Control**

Infants and young children tend to display motor control closer to the trunk and center of the body (proximal) before they can control the finer movements of the wrists, hands, fingers, feet, and toes (distal).

5 **Stationary Position → Locomotor Action**

Babies and very young children generally display more motor control when in a lying or sitting position (stationary) before they can move around and through their environment (locomotion).

6 **Undifferentiated Movement → Differentiated Movement**

A child may bump or fumble with a rattle or toy (undifferentiated movement) before being able to deliberately grasp, shake, or purposely place an object on a table or in a certain location (differentiated movement).

7 **Gross Motor Control → Fine Motor Control**

Most children are able to display control of the large muscles (gross motor) before they show control over small muscles in the hands or feet (fine motor). For example, most children learn to roll over, sit, and crawl before they learn to use a spoon to eat food.

While both gross and fine motor movements involve visual processing, fine motor skills typically require a higher degree of eye-hand coordination because of the precise movements made by the small finger muscles, as in threading beads on a string. In addition, handedness (choosing to use the left or right hand for most fine motor tasks) is acquired slowly, starting around two-and-a-half years of age, and generally becoming more consistent around age four.

> *Regular use of the preferred hand is important for the kindergarten-aged child so that she can learn and practice skills consistently. This consistency helps to establish motor patterns and motor memory over time.*

8 Simple Skills → Complex Skills

Children will find it easier to throw a ball randomly (simple skill) before they are capable of aiming a small ball past a moving and opposing teammate into a narrow goal or net (complex skill).

9 Control of the Body → Control of Objects

A child masters the extension of the leg and hip joints in walking (control of the body) before being able to use the same limbs to kick a ball properly (control of objects). This sequence is the same for the shoulder and arm joints. For example, a child must learn to control the use of the shoulder, elbow, and hand before being able to throw a ball properly. Likewise, ball throwing is typically mastered before the child can use a bat or racquet, which acts as an extension to the arm. That is because controlling and manipulating a badminton racquet is a much more complex skill than simply throwing a ball.

10 Large and Near → Small and Far

Children can manage large objects nearby more effectively and before they can manage smaller objects with distant targets. When first introducing games and equipment to children, the supervising adult should be positioned close to the child and the child should have access to large objects. For example, when first learning to aim a ball at an object, young children do better when rolling a big ball from about four feet away than they do when rolling a Ping-Pong ball from a distance of 20 feet.

11 Stable Environment → Changing Environment

Children generally find it easier to control their movements when maneuvering within or about an unmovable surface (stable environment) than if everything is moving around them (changing environment). For example, walking on the floor is much easier than walking on a trampoline while two other children are bouncing on the mat. Similarly, it is easier to plan a movement response when mounting stable playground equipment than when reacting to a soccer ball in a game with many friends moving around the field.

■ Factors That Impact Motor Skill Development and/or Performance

Many factors can influence the acquisition of motor skills. These factors may impact some people much more or much less than others. The items in the box on page 27 and discussed below can have substantial effects on motor skill development for any child.

> *Many factors can influence the acquisition of motor skills. These factors may impact some people much more or much less than others.*

1 Chronological Age

A child performs motor skills more proficiently with increasing age.

2 Changes in Height and Weight

As children gain height and weight, they tend to become stronger and better able to perform physical activities with more force and control.

Chapter One

Factors That Impact Motor Skill Development

1 Chronological Age

2 Changes in Height and Weight

3 Quantity and Quality of Physical Activity and Play

4 Muscle Strength, Endurance, and Coordination

5 Hand-Eye Coordination

6 Reaction Time

7 Accuracy and Force

8 Posture and Balance

9 Physical Limitations

10 Cognitive Ability

11 Perceptual Motor Skills

12 Visual Processing

13 Proprioceptive-Kinesthetic (PK) Feedback

14 Tactile System

15 Motor Planning

16 Motor Memory

17 Nutrition, Relaxation, and Sleep

18 Medications

19 Environmental Opportunities

20 Family Lifestyle and Expectations

21 Access to Good Performance Models

22 Teaching Style/Learning Style Mismatch

23 Attention

24 History of Failure

Chapter One

3 Quantity and Quality of Physical Activity and Play

The more opportunities children have to engage in varied physical activity and play, the more likely they will find a sport or physical activity they enjoy. When individuals participate in activities they are interested in, their motivation tends to increase and, through ongoing practice, they tend to become competent at those skills or sports.

Gender differences in this area typically become apparent by middle childhood. Although the norms of most assessment tools reveal differences in physical abilities between boys and girls, some research suggests that this is usually more a function of differing cultural expectations than physiological variations at a young age. However, as children reach the pubescent years, the differences between males and females usually become more pronounced.

4 Muscle Strength, Endurance, and Coordination

As children gain muscle mass and strength, joint movement typically becomes more efficient, strength increases, and children gain endurance. This muscle development results in more diverse and coordinated movements.

Coordinated movement involves specific patterns. Each term below describes one of these patterns:

Unilateral is the control of one limb on one side of the body. For instance, a student raises an arm in class to signal the teacher.

Bilateral is controlling the same limbs on the right and left sides of the body in a cooperative or complimentary manner, as when tying shoelaces, clapping hands or performing a bench press with both legs together, doing a jumping jack, or putting beads on a string.

Homo-lateral is controlling the limbs on the same side of the body. For example, a young child learning to throw a ball with the right hand typically steps forward with the same-side foot. Likewise, a teenager lifts his right leg and drops his flexed right arm with fisted hand while shouting "Yes!" during a moment of joy, or an individual steps out and reaches with the right arm and leg while moving along a ropes course.

Cross-lateral is controlling limb action on opposing sides of the body at the same time. A child learning to walk extends and swings the right arm and left leg forward at the same time while the left arm and right leg are both positioned to the back. Without even thinking about it, we naturally tend to run and skip using a cross-lateral movement pattern.

5 Hand-Eye Coordination

As infants become toddlers and young children, they usually become more proficient at using their eyes to coordinate and control hand and foot action. For example, an infant displays hand-eye coordination by looking at a baby bottle of milk while raising it to drink from it. Years later that child may be able to catch a fast-approaching ball because he knows where his hand is in space and in relation to the object. The same thing occurs with kicking. A very young child needs to look at the ball in order to connect with it, but a nine-year-old may only glance at the ball momentarily and then shift his focus to look for someone to pass the ball to on the soccer field before kicking the ball.

6 Reaction Time

The more often a child performs a specific action and the more proficiently she does it, the quicker she can execute the action. Consider the young child learning to kick a ball. This is a slow, careful process and the ball moves rather slowly at first. Once the skill is developed and has become automatic, the youngster can kick the ball very quickly and with a minimal amount of cognitive planning or thought.

7 Accuracy and Force

As children grow and mature, they generally become more accurate in gross motor skills, such as throwing, catching, kicking, and striking. Also, the force with which children carry out various actions usually increases with age due to gains in muscle strength and control. In addition, as children acquire fine motor control, their accuracy in tasks like cutting, coloring, and writing also improves. Furthermore, children usually become more skilled at controlling the amount of force needed to perform a task. In contrast to gross motor actions that become more forceful, as fine motor control develops, the force is generally reduced. For example, a young child usually exerts great pressure on a crayon or pencil when first learning to print or color, yet an adolescent learning to cross-stitch uses delicate, controlled force when inserting thread into an embroidery needle.

8 Posture and Balance

A child who exhibits poor posture and balance is more likely to have difficulty with movement skills than a child who has good balance and posture. The vestibular system is a critical component of posture and balance. This sensory system perceives the effects of gravity and motion as well as the head position and its movements. Tiny hair cell receptors in the inner ear area of the temporal lobe provide the information required for the vestibular system to operate properly.

9 Physical Limitations

A child with a heart murmur, asthma, foot/ankle defect, or any other medical or physical disability will likely have more problems managing sports-related activities than a child with no medical or physical issues.

10 Cognitive Ability

It is not uncommon for a child with low intelligence or cognitive ability to also have some motor difficulties.

> *Several studies have concluded that children with Down syndrome (DS) tend to be more delayed in motor skills than in cognitive skills. When their mental and motor skills are measured on standardized and norm-referenced tests, children with DS tend to show higher scores in their intellectual ability than in their motor abilities.*

Research shows, for example, that a child with Down syndrome (DS) typically moves in a unique manner and has more difficulty with fundamental motor skills than a same-aged peer with no cognitive delay.

11 Perceptual Motor Skills

A student who is able to perceive and understand via sensory input how to move and respond to action experiences will likely be able to make sense of and interact efficiently within the environment. In contrast, a student who does not perceive or know how to react to motion will be much more limited in movement experiences. As such, the student will have more difficulty knowing how and when to respond to moving objects; that same individual may also experience significant problems moving independently through the environment. (Researchers have concluded that beyond the age of five years, the kinesthetic, visual, and auditory registers do not change significantly.)

12 Visual Processing

Visual processing means recognizing and making sense of visual information. Efficient visual processing is required for most motor tasks, especially those involving hand-eye or foot-eye coordination. It also allows one to judge distances and to track the movement of objects. Visual processing also allows one to discriminate among various symbols, letters, numbers, and shapes, such as these:

A H ϒ ^ 4 Z K N Æ Λ Ê

Ê Z F J °Ê B $ 5 Ä S T

A student with ineffective visual processing might have problems recognizing that the following all represent the same letter of the alphabet:

A a 𝒜 **A** a 𝒜 A a **A a** a A 𝐴 **A a** A

Ineffective visual processing can impact a student's ability to discern what is happening and to respond quickly and appropriately to information in the environment. For example, someone might view the word *STOP* as $ + O Ρ and, as a result, not react as expected. In addition, children who have difficulty with depth perception may bump into others or misjudge distances and not react to changes in the environment as efficiently as others.

13 Proprioceptive-Kinesthetic (PK) Feedback

Proprioceptive-kinesthetic (PK) feedback refers to the ability to know where your body or body parts are in space when you are moving or stationary. Furthermore, PK feedback allows you to sense the force, speed, space, and timing of your movements. This information is sent from receptors in your muscles, tendons, and joints up to your brain and informs you about different aspects of motion, such as resistance, compression, traction, elongation, active and passive movements, and stretching.

To test for PK feedback, close your eyes and consider where your arms and legs are. Are they crossed or resting on an object? Alternatively, let someone position one of your limbs in different ways. Then try to duplicate that position by imitating that motion with your other limb.

You can also test for PK feedback on your own. If you can walk down a dark hallway at home at night and know exactly where to place your hand to turn on the bathroom light switch, you have fairly good PK feedback. Likewise, if you are asked to position your right palm upward at a 45° angle behind your right hip at about the height of a kitchen table, and you can do that within a height of seven inches, your PK feedback is also very good.

14 Tactile System

The tactile (touch) system is embedded in the skin. The receptors for the tactile system sense deep pressure, heat, pain, cold, various textures, and other types of touch, such as a tender kiss on the lips. Research has shown that many children who have motor difficulties may also have problems discriminating differences among various objects when limited to just feeling these objects with their hands.

15 Motor Planning

Effective motor planning involves executing an action in the proper order or sequence. For example, if asked to throw a ball, a student should know that it is important to take a step forward just before raising the throwing arm and releasing the ball. In addition, if required to do a two-foot jump, the student should know that to prepare, it is important to bend the knees while bending and swinging both arms – then, while thrusting the arms forward and upward, the student should push off the floor, extending the legs as quickly as possible. Any other combination of the motor plan would yield a very awkward, inefficient motion.

16 Motor Memory

A student who has strong motor memory and enough experience will be able to recreate a motor engram (pattern) the same way every time. For example, an adult should be able to reproduce her signature exactly the same way with her eyes open or closed (see diagram below).

Adult's signature (reasonably good motor memory)

eyes open: *eyes closed:*

Lisa Parker   *Lisa Parker*

Child's signature (poor motor memory)

eyes open: *eyes closed:*

Danny Whiskeyman   *Danny Whiskeyman*

Chapter One

As an example of a gross motor task involving motor memory, a basketball player should be able to stand at the free throw line and, with eyes closed, know how to stand, how much force to apply, when to release the ball, and when to expect to hear the ball hit the backboard/rim before it drops through the hoop.

17 Nutrition, Relaxation, and Sleep

Common sense tells us that good rest and nutrition will enhance motor skill performance. On the other hand, sleep deprivation and long-term poor dietary habits or allergies can negatively impact reaction time and the ability to plan motor responses. That is why many coaches implement very strict guidelines for their athletes in the areas of sleep and nutrition.

There is very interesting literature that suggests many individuals do not realize they have allergies to foods. One simple way to sense whether you might have allergies is to note how intensely and frequently you have a craving for similar food group items per week. Often that is a substance you are allergic to!

18 Medications

Drugs and medicines can alter one's movement capabilities. Sleeping pills, alcohol, muscle relaxants, and other sedatives generally reduce motor skill performance. However, some medications are known to enhance motor skills for a period of time. Check with your medical doctor and/or pharmacist for the possible effects of your child's medication on motor skill performances.

19 Environmental Opportunities

Children who have had a great deal of exposure to playground equipment, recreational sports, indoor or outdoor play activities, and other similar environments will likely be more proficient at gross motor skills than children who have not had the same opportunities.

20 Family Lifestyle and Expectations

If parents generally expect their child to join them on long walks in the neighborhood; to go bicycle riding, swimming, or skating as a family; or participate in other similar activities, their child will likely be more proficient at physical activities than another youngster who has spent most of his leisure time indoors playing board and card games with his family or playing video games all alone. Likewise, a child who has had many opportunities to play board games, help with cooking and baking tasks in the kitchen, and do puzzles and crafts is likely more proficient at fine motor tasks than a youngster who is usually outdoors. As always, a good balance of all types of experiences and skills is best.

21 Access to Good Performance Models

If a child has parents, relatives, teachers, or coaches who are very proficient at sports and physical activities, it is likely that the child has received some basic instruction from these adults at some point. On the other hand, if parents and other adult caregivers are not exceptional at sports, and, as a result, are unsure how to teach the child certain skills, the child's motor skills are probably not as well developed. Once again, there may also be parents who are skilled at fixing or assembling computers and other electronic appliances, model building, sewing, beading, and other types of fine motor skill recreational pursuits. Their children may become more proficient at fine motor tasks than gross motor activities.

22 Teaching Style/Learning Style Mismatch

Some children learn best by verbal or visual methods while others need kinesthetic cues or a combination of the strategies just listed. If an adult typically uses only one method to teach a child motor skills and this method does not match the child's preferred learning modality, then the child is at a disadvantage in learning.

23 Attention

A student who has any one of the three main types of attention problems may have impaired ability to perform various motor skills. A child diagnosed with attention deficit/hyperactivity disorder (AD/HD) of the primarily hyperactive/impulsive type may actually be quite good at many sports because he seems to have a natural need to move. However, many of these children bump into objects and appear clumsy because of their impulsive and spontaneous natures.

In contrast, children who are diagnosed with AD/HD of the primarily inattentive type may not be as skilled in certain gross motor activities because they are more apt to daydream or to be content to sit and watch others rather than join activities.

It is difficult to guess what type of motor skills a child with the third type of AD/HD (combined hyperactive/impulsive and inattentive type) will display because different features of the AD/HD may be noticeable at various times. Nevertheless, be aware that sometimes a child with clumsy behaviors may not actually have motor skill difficulties; it simply looks that way because the child is not paying proper attention to the environment.

> *Sometimes a child with clumsy behaviors may not actually have motor skill difficulties; it simply looks that way because the child is not paying proper attention to the environment.*

24 History of Failure

Children who are skilled at performing various motor skills tend to engage in these and similar activities on a regular basis. This repeated performance increases their expertise. In contrast, children who have lower motor skill proficiency may perceive themselves as incompetent and, therefore, may participate less often in various physical activities. This lack of participation naturally results in reduced mastery attempts, and these children will be less efficient and successful in their movement experiences.

Ongoing failure has an enormous impact on a child's psychosocial development. Because this is such an important topic, this subject will be expanded on in subsequent chapters throughout this book.

Chapter One

■ Summary

Motor skill development is a fascinating process that typically follows an orderly progression. These various stages were researched and documented many years ago, and the progression remains rather steady and constant, even with other complex changes in our society. Each child may progress through the various developmental steps at a slightly different rate and in a somewhat different order.

Not all children who experience motor difficulties do so because of the same conditions or problems. Rather, many factors can alter the course of motor skill acquisition. Some of these impact one person more than another, and certain situations are very difficult to address and change. However, some factors can be altered and require a purposeful adjustment in lifestyle, habits, interests, and attitude to reach a desired result. It is beneficial to learn and practice all types of gross and fine motor skills.

Understanding how motor skills develop and what factors can positively or negatively affect that development enables us to determine with more certainty the different skills that are problematic in a particular child. Such knowledge allows us to ask basic questions about what, if anything, can be done at home and/or in school to reduce motor problems. Always consider these questions before consulting a medical doctor or other professional.

Chapter One

■ References

- Bayley, N. (1993). *Bayley scales of infant development (2nd ed.).* San Antonio, TX: Therapy Skill Builders.

- Bruner, J. (1973). Organization of early skilled action. *Child Development, 44*(1), 1-11. In D.L. Gallahue & J.C. Ozmun (Eds.), *Understanding motor development: Infants, children, adolescents, adults (3rd ed.).* Dubuque, IA: WCB Brown & Benchmark Publishers.

- Burton, A.E., & Miller, D.E. (1998). *Movement skill assessment.* Champaign, IL: Human Kinetics Publishers, Inc.

- Gesell, A. (1925). *The mental growth of the preschool child: A psychological outline of normal development from birth to the sixth year, including a system of developmental diagnosis.* New York: Macmillan Publishers.

- Gesell, A., & Amatruda, C.S. (1941). *Developmental diagnosis: The evaluation and management of normal and abnormal neuropsychological development in infant and early childhood.* New York: P.B. Hoeber, Inc.

- Haywood, K.M., & Getchell, N. (2004). *Life span motor development (4th ed.).* Champaign, IL: Human Kinetics Publishers, Inc.

- Keogh, J. (1977). The study of movement skill development. *Quest, 28,* 76-88.

- Keogh, J.F., & Sugden, D.A. (1985). *Movement skill development.* New York: Macmillan Publishers.

- Moran, J.M., & Kalakian, L.H. (1977). *Movement experiences for the mentally retarded or emotionally disturbed child (2nd ed.).* Minneapolis, MN: Burgess Publishing Company.

- Rarick, G.L. (1961). *Motor development during infancy and childhood (Rev. ed.).* Madison, WI: College Printing and Typing.

- Rice, F.P. (1995). *Human development: A lifespan approach (2nd ed.).* Englewood Cliffs, NJ: Prentice-Hall, Inc.

Chapter One

- Sherrill, C. (1977). *Adapted physical education and recreation: A multi-disciplinary approach.* Dubuque, IA: Wm. C. Brown Company Publishers.

- Sherrill, C. (1993). *Adapted physical activity, recreation, and sport: Crossdisciplinary and lifespan (4th ed.).* Dubuque, IA: Wm. C. Brown Company Publishers.

- Sugden, D.A., & Keogh, J.F. (1990). Problems in movement skill development. In H.G. Williams (Ed.), *Growth, motor development, and physical activity across the lifespan.* Columbia, SC: University of South Carolina Press.

- Thomas, J.R. (1984). *Motor development through childhood and adolescence.* Minneapolis, MN: Burgess Publishing Company.

- Wickstrom, R.L. (1983). *Fundamental motor patterns (3rd ed.).* Philadelphia, PA: Lea & Febiger.

The Source for DCD　　　　39

Chapter Two

This chapter presents information about three important topics:

1 **A Detective at Work – Initial Clues**

   Due to the nature of their work with very young children, speech-language therapists or pathologists (SLPs) may be one of the first professionals to notice motor irregularities in your child. That is because there are close ties between speech problems and other motor difficulties. You will also read descriptions of some of the behaviors an SLP may notice.

2 **The Effect of Poor Motor Coordination on Psychosocial Development**

   Weak or delayed motor skills impact the psychosocial development of children and young adults. It is very important to find, diagnose, and provide intervention to address these motor difficulties in young children because of the impact of poor motor skills on other domains of behavior.

3 **Checklists for Motor Skill Difficulties**

   This chapter includes comprehensive checklists of motor skills. By identifying the motor skills that are problematic in your child, you will understand whether or not you need to be concerned. If so, follow-up by scheduling an appointment with a specialist to have any motor difficulties investigated further.

■ A Detective at Work – Initial Clues

Many young children have some type of delay or difficulty in acquiring motor, speech, and/or social skills during the first years of life. Concerned parents typically meet with their doctors, who usually then refer these parents and their children to other healthcare professionals. One group of service providers who interact with many preschool-aged children are SLPs. These skilled individuals are in a very privileged position to detect special needs or developmental delays in addition to speech and language issues.

By identifying these youngsters early, an SLP may actually facilitate the process of early diagnosis and intervention of other conditions. For example, research reveals that 50% or more children with speech and language disorders also have other motor difficulties because, like most gross and fine motor skills, speech requires planning and control. Specifically, speech involves a complex inter-action of precise manipulation of muscles in the mouth, breath support and control, and other oral motor movements.

Chapter Two

If you observe, for instance, that, along with speech problems, a child's skills and abilities in fine and/or gross motor tasks are much weaker than would be expected for her age and apparent intellectual ability, and you feel that the obvious motor problems are not due to some type of a medical condition(s), this child may have an identifiable disorder. Information within the *DSM-IV-TR* states that motor coordination problems are often associated with speech and language difficulties:

> 66 Problems commonly associated with DCD include delays in other non-motor milestones. Associated disorders may include Phonological Disorder, Expressive Language Disorder, and Mixed Receptive-Expressive Language Disorder" (p. 57). 99 [1]

◆ ◆ ◆

An SLP's warning bells should sound if a child exhibits these behaviors:

- late talker

- dysfluent speech

- oral motor and/or articulation concerns

- problems pronouncing word syllables in the correct order

- specific problems with word retrieval

- difficulty planning and constructing sentences

- slightly delayed in achieving motor milestones and/or resists various tabletop activities (e.g., drawing or manipulating game pieces)

- poor or slouched posture or wiggly and squirmy behaviors when sitting

- difficulty positioning himself on a chair and/or organizing himself at a table

---

[1] Reprinted with permission from the *Diagnostic and Statistical Manual of Mental Disorders, Text Revision*, Copyright 2000. American Psychiatric Association.

Chapter Two

- trouble coordinating tasks that require using both hands (e.g., threading beads or stabilizing paper when drawing or cutting)

- limp hand action or extreme pressure when manipulating objects or writing

- poor pencil grip and very weak, inconsistent printing and/or writing skills

- performs motor actions in ways that are much different from same-aged peers (e.g., throwing and catching, running, jumping))

- appears delayed, clumsy, or awkward in motor behaviors

◆ ◆ ◆

In addition, the SLP may notice that, when working with these children, she frequently does these things to help:

- offers hand-over-hand help

- finishes tasks in order to speed things up or as a way to save the child from embarrassment

- helps the child with dressing (e.g., buttoning up sweaters, zipping up jackets, helping with putting shoes on the proper feet, fastening Velcro closures or tying laces)

- unconsciously helps move chairs in and out of the proper position for the child

- stabilizes papers or other objects so the child can perform certain tasks

- provides more help to these children than to other boys and girls of the same age

◆ ◆ ◆

Chapter Two

If so, the child you are working with may have a specific motor coordination disorder. You would do well to ask parents questions about their child's ability to perform various motor skills. In addition to the other items listed elsewhere in this chapter, you could start with simple questions about motor skills normally acquired during ages three to six, such as these:

- Does your child have the ability to get dressed independently?

- Does your child have the basic skills to manage pencils, crayons, scissors, glue, etc.?

- Is your child proficient when using a knife, fork, and spoon?

- Does your child have the ability to perform kitchen skills such as pouring liquids, buttering bread, opening juice boxes, cutting waffles, etc.?

- Is your child able to ride a tricycle or bicycle?

- Does your child have any involvement or interest in team sports and games?

◆ ◆ ◆

What can you do as an SLP once you recognize some of these concerns about a child? If parental concerns match your clinical observations, you might suggest that the parents schedule an appointment with a professional who knows about general motor coordination problems. You might even suggest that the parents seek help from an occupational or physical therapist (OT or PT) who can assess the child's motor skills. Unfortunately, OTs and PTs are unable to make a definitive diagnosis because motor skill difficulties are also indicative of other disorders, so the parents will also need to visit a developmental pediatrician, psychiatrist, or psychologist who has experience in the motor area in order to obtain a diagnosis.

Once a diagnosis is made, encourage the parents to become educated about the topic and to use whatever resources are available to learn what types of intervention will make a positive difference for their child.

Chapter Two

■ **The Effect of Poor Motor Coordination on Psychosocial Development**

When a child, youth, or adolescent has problems with motor coordination, it can have far-reaching implications. This relationship is confirmed by research and should cause parents, teachers, therapists, doctors, psychiatrists, and psychologists great concern. Studies have shown that as children with motor learning difficulties go through school, often even before they reach adolescence, they tend to experience significant emotional difficulties. This development is likely the result of reduced interpersonal relationships, ongoing sadness and disappointment, and other negative feelings and situations from earlier years.

Consider the following story. Note how young this child is when he already starts to feel the pain of being unable to perform motor skills at the same speed and with the same ability as his peers. In essence, it is an example of how motor problems develop into psychosocial difficulties.

Marco is four years old. It is a hot summer day, and even though it is only 11:00 A.M., Marco and his mother, Angelina, have decided to have a picnic lunch at a shady park near their home. They have done this several other times during the last few months, and Marco is excited! Earlier today, Angelina's boss at the landscaping service company had informed her that she did not need to come in because of equipment problems. What a pleasant surprise!

While Marco watches, his mother packs two pastrami wraps, some carrots, two mangoes, one large chocolate bar, and a thermos with ice-cold lemonade. She also packs a large purple blanket, a red rubber ball, the novel she is reading, and their sunglasses. Then Angelina invites Marco to hold her hand as she slings her large bag over her left shoulder. She locks the apartment door and they walk down the hallway together.

Angelina lets Marco press the button for the elevator and smiles as he looks up at the buttons indicating the movement of the elevator in the building. Then in order, like every other day, the green light shines brightly just before the bell rings and the elevator door slowly opens. They enter the elevator and, within minutes, exit four stories below into the apartment lobby.

They turn left as they leave the building and head to the bus stop down the street. After a short wait and a ten-minute bus ride, Marco and Angelina arrive at their destination. They descend the stairs of the bus and walk hand-in-hand for about four or five more minutes until they are close to the playground equipment.

There are many others at the park today. Angelina looks around, decides she wants to sit under a large tree, and then takes the hefty tote bag off her shoulder and places it on the ground. Next she spreads out the big purple blanket; gives Marco his sunglasses and hat; covers his face, arms, and ears with sunscreen; and sits down while Marco looks around.

He sees lots of other boys and girls playing on the swings, slide, wooden jungle gym, and other playground equipment. In particular, Marco's eyes are drawn to the big, red, curly slide because there are several other children about his age playing there. He notices that the children look like they are chasing each other up and down the slide. "Oh, boy," Marco thinks. "It looks like fun and I want to try it, too!"

With his mom's permission and encouragement, Marco slowly wanders toward the playground and the slide. He was here last Saturday morning, too, when his dad came for a visit. It was cold and windy that day and there were no other children around. His dad had helped him get on the swings and go down what he called the "spaghetti" slide a few times. It was fun. Marco wants to try that slide again.

He starts to make his way over to the slide's ladder but stops a short distance before it and looks up. It is big and tall and he's not sure he can climb it by himself, so he glances back at his mom to see if she will help him. By now, though, she seems to have settled in and is already reading her book. Marco really wants to go down the slide. He thinks maybe he can do it alone now. After all, his dad had just helped him last week and he had also tried it with his mom a few times before that. He decides to start by trying to climb the ladder.

Marco takes another ten steps forward and stands at the bottom of the ladder. Although he is now waiting for his turn to climb it, other children push past him and climb much faster. He stands back a little because they are going so fast! He looks back at Mom, who has just glanced up to look at him. She waves, and Marco smiles and waves back. He thinks, "Okay, I will show Mom that I can slide by myself."

Marco steps forward and tries to put his hands on the edge of the ladder so he can climb up, but one girl sneaks right under his arms and races up the ladder. Marco lifts one leg to take a step on the ladder. A bigger boy behind him is already telling him to hurry up. Marco steps down and stands back once more.

After waiting a few minutes until the children have moved onto some other playground equipment, Marco steps forward again and places his hands on the edge of the ladder. He turns to see how many other children are near him. No one! Marco lifts his right leg and places it on the first step again. Then he lifts the other leg and places it beside the right leg. He moves his hands up the edge of the ladder just a little and holds on very tightly. Then he lifts his right leg again and positions it very carefully on the second step. His progress up the slide is very slow, and by the time he has both feet on the third rung of the ladder, two children are pushing each other just below him.

Marco starts to panic. Although he wants to turn around to see what is going on behind him, he needs to use all his energy to hold onto the ladder and figure out which step to take next. He is starting to get scared and he has three more steps to climb! Those will take longer and now the children are starting to shout, "Hurry up! Get going, slowpoke! What's taking you so long?"

Marco knows he must concentrate very hard to keep going up the steps, and because he wants to prove to his mom and himself that he can do it, he continues. By the time he makes it to the top platform of the slide, he is really scared and can feel the other children pushing on his back.

With all the courage he can muster, Marco takes his time sitting down, positioning his legs properly, and then grabbing the sides of the slide. Now he must focus and remember to hold onto the slide so he will not go too fast. His dad told him that just last week.

Chapter Two

Chapter Two

Marco edges forward on the slide and makes the descent. He is petri-fied and ends up sliding a bit too fast, going round and round and then losing his balance at the bottom. He falls over and lands hard on his buttocks and hands. The little rocks hurt his hands. Marco gets up, rubs his hands on his legs, and then runs to Angelina. He doesn't want to go down the slide again, especially when other children are around. He just wants to sit close to his mom where it is safe.

Three years later, Marco is attending school full-time. His mom often comments about how he has grown bigger and stronger and how Grannie and Poppa will notice that when they come to visit. Marco can't wait to see them because other things aren't too exciting anymore. His mom has a boyfriend now, and Marco only sees his dad a few times each month. They have good times then, but his dad always asks the same questions, like, "How's school? What have you learned and been doing since the last time I saw you?"

Overall, Marco thinks that school is kind of all right. He is a good reader and knows a lot of answers when the teacher asks questions, but he hates printing and his teacher always makes him do it over so it won't look so messy. "Doesn't she know I've already done my best?" he wonders.

Everyone makes him print and color and cut and paste. He has to do it at school and then a lady comes and makes him play with little things and practice printing. Then sometimes his mom makes him do it at home, too, before he gets to watch TV. He is starting to hate that part of school.

Usually he thinks it is pretty fun to go into the gym with his classmates when they have physical education class. Sometimes they get to do things like "move as close to the floor as possible," "be as skinny as possible when you move," or "glide slowly like a bird." He likes those days because he can do those things.

Other days he must do activities with a partner. Then he wishes he were sick. The teacher might tell them to run as fast as possible, throw and catch a ball with a friend, or play scoop ball together. He doesn't like those days because he hardly ever gets it right.

Chapter Two

Marco starts to get nervous when the teacher says, "Please find a partner." No one ever comes up to him to ask him to be his partner, and he usually ends up waiting for the teacher to pair him with someone. Most of the time the other person is not very good at doing the activities either, and so, even though the two of them try to do the activities, they are often chasing the ball or some other object around the gym floor because they both keep missing it. "Most children are throwing and catching about 100 times," thinks Marco, while he and his partner only do it about five times. "It's hard to get good at it when you hardly ever get to practice," Marco tells himself.

Three years later, Marco is in fifth grade. He's starting to have a very tough time at school. He doesn't like unit studies or group work or math or most other subjects. The only subjects that are half good are language arts and science. He hates P.E. Whenever he has to go to P.E., he only gets the old leftover balls and other equipment – like the dirty, old rackets with the strings hanging out or the balls that are half flat and any other stuff no one else will touch.

Marco usually stands near a corner and tries to look busy so the P.E. teacher won't hassle him, but he really can't stand coming to this class. Often he tries to pretend that he is sick so that he can sit on the bench. Sometimes the teacher makes him participate, but other times she just lets him sit there.

Deep inside, Marco still wants to learn the sports stuff because everybody else talks about it and does it during recess and lunch break, but he really doesn't "get it." It's frustrating to want to learn how to do some of the activities when your body won't work that way. "Oh, well. Thank goodness today is the last day of the week," Marco thinks to himself.

Marco just remembered that he did pretty well on the science quiz today. He will bring it home and show his mom. Tomorrow is Saturday and Marco hopes he doesn't have to go to those stupid swimming lessons that his mom signed him up for.

Chapter Two

Marco is now in seventh grade. Middle school. There are lots of teachers and big kids walking around the hallways during breaks; even the girls in his class are bigger than he is! He's pretty shy now and doesn't hang around with the cool kids. As a matter of fact, he doesn't really hang out with anyone. He is glad that the breaks between classes are short. Recess the last few years had really started to get embarrassing – he would just find a spot to sit down on the school stairs and stay there the whole 15 minutes. No one ever asked him to join in a soccer game or shoot baskets or play touch football.

Lunch breaks were worse. Marco used to walk around near the doors of the school, lean on the school wall in a shady spot, or hang around the supervisors. Now he sometimes makes his way to the picnic benches near the skateboard ramp and leans on the tree closest to the picnic table. That makes him feel like he is kind of close to the action. Still, no one ever bothers to talk to him.

Still, no one ever bothers to talk to him.

Marco overhears his classmates talking about calling each other on the phone tonight, but he can't remember the last time a classmate called him to talk. Usually when the phone rings, it's for his mom. Sometimes he talks to Grannie. She is lonely, too, now that she lives alone. She kind of knows how he feels. Otherwise, the phone is pretty quiet at night.

Marco isn't looking forward to the summer much, either. There isn't a whole lot to do at home except watch TV and play computer or video games. "Oh, well," he thinks, "I wonder what's for supper? Maybe Mom will make some of that great creamy beef cannelloni again. I'm so hungry that I'm going to have two or maybe three helpings. Then one of my favorite shows comes on. Maybe it will be an okay night after all."

Marco is finally in high school. He does well on the computer, and once in a while some classmates ask him for help with their computer problems. Angelina is encouraging him to follow a career path with computers because he is so good at it. It also happens to be one of the only things that Marco has an interest in.

Chapter Two

While wandering through the school halls at lunch one day, Marco overhears some kids talking about the big basketball game against Riverbend High School. It will start right after classes are done today. He would like to go watch the game, but he knows he would just end up sitting by himself.

Marco decides to go home instead. "It will be another long and boring night, just doing the same old computer stuff at home that I did today at school. Then tomorrow at school, I'll just do what I end up doing tonight at home. My life sure isn't much fun. I'm really starting to believe that maybe the world would be a better place if I were gone. I don't think anyone but Mom would miss me anyway. She's got a new boyfriend again, so maybe this guy would take care of her. She sure isn't spending a lot of time with me anymore. Actually, I don't know if Mom would miss me as much as I would hope. She'd get over it in time – that's what she's always telling me to do." And so Marco's thoughts drift aimlessly each day.

What started out as a motor coordination problem has affected his confidence, self-esteem, willingness to take age-appropriate risks, participation in healthy activities, and peer interactions. Marco is a sad, lonely, angry person. He doesn't do much physical activity anymore, and rewards himself with food and sedentary activities. As a result, the poor motor coordination is affecting Marco's early scholastic experience as well as his psychosocial, emotional, and physical health.

> Marco is a sad, lonely, angry person.

What's next for Marco? Why didn't anyone recognize his difficulties? Why didn't someone step in earlier and offer some help? And what kind of help should Marco have been given?

◆　◆　◆

Chapter Two

We may or may not know anyone like Marco who, at age three or four, has (or had) significant motor delays, yet I am almost certain that each one of us can think back to our own days at school and remember the classmates who were the last students picked for teams in P.E. You may have even been one of them. You may or may not recall that some of these same students stood by the school wall all alone during recess and lunch breaks. You may have even had a fleeting thought such as, "These kids sure don't have many friends to play with."

Research findings confirm this pattern. Studies show that children who have average to above-average intelligence but who have problems learning motor skills, often display academic underachievement and difficulties with peer relationships. These children also tend to have low self-esteem and poor self-concept, and they sometimes display other emotional disorders.

Several researchers have studied and applied various theories to explain how motor development and learning relates to psychological and social development. For example, the competence motivation theory describes what happens over time when children struggle with learning and performing motor skills. One assumption of this theory is that the major goal of achievement is feeling competent and developing a level of mastery. These researchers suggest that if a child thinks or perceives she is competent at a particular activity, this thought will promote ongoing interest in the activity and continued attempts to master the skill. On the other hand, if a child perceives herself as incompetent, she will naturally limit her participation, resulting in reduced mastery attempts.

Just think about it. For example, if the first time you tried golf you were encouraged and felt that you played okay, you might have been interested in trying it again. In contrast, if you had a lousy experience and felt embarrassed by the number of tries it took you to sink the ball into the cup while others watched and waited, you might have decided you didn't need to subject yourself to such public humiliation again.

Research has shown that children with poor or delayed motor skills see themselves as having low athletic ability, reduced scholastic skills when compared with their peers, and a less desirable physical appearance.

Chapter Two

In much the same way, because of repeated failure when performing motor skills, children with poor coordination generally experience low levels of competency in the motor domain. They start to avoid participation in activities because they fear further failure and the associated peer criticism. As a result, they have fewer practice opportunities and reduced social interaction. As these children develop reduced feelings of competence in the motor domain, it is common for them to also formulate a diminished self-perception and to feel less capable in other areas as well. Research has shown that children with poor or delayed motor skills see themselves as having low athletic ability, reduced scholastic skills when compared with their peers, and a less desirable physical appearance. It follows that the children then withdraw from social settings to prevent further feelings of failure.

Self-worth is usually related to two main factors: acceptance from others and perceived achievements (and the importance an individual places on them). If a student feels very inadequate in skills that most others the same age feel are important, feelings of incompetence can progress to reduced global self-worth, a negative view of oneself, shyness, withdrawal, sadness, and possibly depression. For the student with motor skill difficulties without intervention and support, this negative spiral paints a very grim picture indeed.

In addition, research shows that if a child has reduced motor ability and receives negative input and comments from significant others and peers, over time, this can influence the child's health and wellness. Common consequences include a poor self-concept, feelings of ineptitude, and a fear of participation. Left untreated, the child may develop anxiety and depression, both major mental health concerns. In addition, a sedentary lifestyle with limited physical activity may also lead to weight gain and associated physical and mental health concerns.

To combat this devastating cycle, parents and professionals should take the following steps.

Step 1: Determine what is causing the motor problems.

Step 2: Seek professional opinions, guidance, and support.

Step 3: Enroll the child in appropriate programs or establish interventions that promote increased motor competency in culturally relevant skills along with opportunities for social interactions.

Note: This last step should occur away from scrutiny of more athletically capable peers.

Chapter Two

Over time and with proper support, intervention, and assistance – conducted in a considerate and purposeful manner – improvements in perceived competence and achievements may result. Once a student has gained an increased sense of motor ability, the child may feel more acceptance from peers, which usually leads to improved self-concept.

If success continues, the student may begin to be less worried about fear of failure, be willing to participate in various motor skill activities, and therefore increase mastery attempts. With continued gains in motor skill abilities, anxiety and depression will likely diminish, feelings of competence may increase, mental and physical health concerns will likely decrease, and the student will experience increased overall self-worth.

■ Checklists for Motor Skill Difficulties

▶ General Information

This section provides checklists including examples of many different motor skills. Remember that all children with motor difficulties do not exhibit the same problems, and motor skill performances can be very inconsistent. Furthermore, it is quite common for typically developing children to have problems in a few of the motor skills listed. Do not be alarmed, therefore, if you check off four or five of the skills identified. Nevertheless, if your child exhibits problems with *most* of the motor skills identified on the following pages, you will probably want to schedule an appointment with a medical professional. If 15 to 20 items seem difficult for your child, student, or client, trust your intuition about whether this is a major concern. Then determine if there is any pattern to the types of difficulties the child has before scheduling a visit with a doctor. Also, before getting overly concerned, review the information in the previous chapter. It may be that the child lacks proper sleep, has poor nutrition, or is experiencing a teaching/learning style mismatch. On the other hand, if you have unconsciously been doing many activities for your child, he or she may simply not have had the opportunity or experience required to learn and do the various tasks and activities with efficiency. You may need to sit and observe your son or daughter over several days to a week to see what your child is capable of doing without the assistance of an adult.

Most of the examples on the checklists will seem straightforward, while other items, a few of which were described in the previous chapter, may identify certain motor skills you have never thought about.

Chapter Two

One way or another, if you come to recognize any patterns in your child's motor skill performances, make the changes you can first (based on the comments in Chapter One). Then, if you still have major concerns, contact your medical professional when you are ready.

Keep in mind, motor skill difficulties can be manifested in numerous ways. Some children may have problems primarily with gross motor skills while others may have difficulty when required to do activities using fingers, hands, and wrists (fine motor skills). It is also possible to have difficulties with other types of motor skills, such as oral motor or toileting skills.

Pages 55-56 and 60-69 present two checklists of common motor skill behaviors. The first checklist is directed primarily at parents as it has to do with the preschool years. The second checklist is geared for school-aged children. Most of the activities listed are what a student would typically perform at home or in school.

Check off each item that applies to the child you live or work with. Mark an item only if the child shows the difficulties consistently and differently from most of the child's same-aged peers.

If you are a doctor or medical professional, you may also want to use the following checklist(s) as part of a more detailed interview with parents.

Preschool Motor Skills Checklist

Check each item that described or describes the child as an infant or a toddler.

▶ Oral-Motor Speech Skills

❏ unable to suck liquids properly and quickly

❏ awkward when drinking from a baby bottle or cup, experiences difficulties coordinating breathing, drinking, and swallowing

❏ excessively messy when eating or drinking

❏ somewhat delayed in speech development and in learning to communicate with others

❏ unclear in pronouncing many words, making it difficult for relatives and neighbors to understand (even if the parent can understand)

▶ Body Position and Movement

❏ slightly delayed in rolling, sitting up, crawling, standing, and/or learning to walk

❏ much slower and less capable than peers when moving around, on, or through playground equipment

❏ needs your help when walking on or climbing over uneven surfaces

❏ somewhat slow when learning to get on and off large toys and playground equipment

❏ has more accidents and mishaps than other same-aged children, resulting in numerous bumps, bruises, or broken limbs

continued on next page

❏ uncoordinated – as though the child is going to fall over when walking quickly, running, or moving up and down inclined surfaces

❏ clumsy, frequently bumping into objects, spilling drinks, or knocking things over

❏ reluctant or unable to ride a large plastic riding toy by using the feet/legs to move forward

❏ runs or jumps with a flat or heavy foot and stiff or jerky action

❏ exhibits a unique or different gait compared to other children the same age

❏ has problems learning to go up and down stairs one step at a time

❏ has difficulty with various tasks involving balance, such as walking along a narrow curb

▶ Fine Motor Skills ••

❏ excessively messy when drawing or coloring

❏ drops hand-held items for no apparent reason

▶ Self-Help Skills ••

❏ slower than others to learn toileting skills

❏ has trouble learning to blow the nose properly (coordinating breathing, holding a tissue, and exhaling through the nose when prompted)

▶ General Attitude ••

❏ less inclined to explore the environment than other children the same age

❏ generally more settled and content than other children the same age

❏ very cautious and possibly even afraid when around energetic, boisterous children

❏ frightened or turns away when a ball or other fast-moving object approaches

❏ unwilling or unable to perform motor tasks that require a quick or accurate response, such as stacking blocks or responding to a rolling ball

The Source for DCD   56

Chapter Two

▶ School-Aged Motor Skills Checklist

The quality and quantity of motor skills change gradually from infancy and toddlerhood to the preschool, kindergarten, and early elementary student. The items in the following checklist focus on motor skills that are more typical of a school-aged child. These skills are not presented in a developmental sequence; instead, they are grouped by various settings or contexts.

Because of diversity in children with motor problems, again, remember that your child or client may actually be able to do a few skills that are generally performed by a much older child. However, if you determine that your twelve-year-old child, for example, is only able to perform basic motor skills, you will now become more alert to the specific motor skill difficulties your child has. This type of information is very valuable for the healthcare professional you may meet eventually.

Since preadolescent and adolescent students often do physical activities with others in various recreational settings or in P.E. classes, some of the following checklist could be completed by a coach or P.E. teacher, classroom teacher, close relative, or family friend who knows the student very well. Few parents have the opportunity to observe their children in different structured group settings, so it may be valuable to have more than one person complete the checklist independently. This approach should provide a comprehensive, objective perspective of each student's skills and abilities.

Few parents have the opportunity to observe their children in different structured group settings, so it may be valuable to have more than one person complete the checklist independently.

Make sure you inform each person completing the checklist that it is part of an informal assessment that may lead to identification of a specific motor problem.

The first section of the checklist covers skills related to motor actions in the following areas:

- Ball Skills

- Balance Activities

- Sports and Recreation

- Personal Care and Hygiene

- Household Tasks

- Kitchen and Food Preparation

- Tabletop Activities

- School Skills and Other Fine Motor Activities

- Other Gross Motor Activities

The second section of the checklist addresses general characteristics of students with motor coordination difficulties. Some items describe individual features and/or general classroom activities, while others relate to students within their peer groups, as in physical education or high school elective classes.

- General Characteristics

- Limited Body Awareness

- Reduced Motivation to Participate in Active Events

- Poor Motor Organization and Planning

- Penmanship

- Resistant Attitude

   Note: When dealing with a child who resists activities, be thoughtful. Remember that if a student is told to perform tasks that he cannot manage or do, that student will often react very sharply in front of his peers. Teachers and parents must be astute and watch very closely for these challenging, disruptive behaviors.

Chapter Two

If the student acts out and then is treated with harsh discipline without the adult realizing that the student may have an underlying motor difficulty, it will result in devastating consequences for the student. That is because the reprimand is for something the student has little control over, especially at the present time. In response, the student may continue to create significant problems for the teacher. Rather, take some time to understand what is really happening for the student.

Ask your co-workers, call the student's parents, and talk to the individual privately. It may be that the cause of the disruptive behavior is totally unrelated to motor skill performances (e.g., difficulties within the peer group, living in a home where there is financial or marital strain, a sudden change in the student's medical health). Once you understand why the student is acting out, you will be in a better position to know what issues must be addressed publicly and when and if certain disciplinary measures are likely to be effective.

Once again, based on your pattern of answers on the following checklist and how significantly these items appear to affect your child's functioning at home and school, you may or may not need to meet with a professional who is able to investigate this further.

Student   _____

Age   _____

Grade   _____

Date   _____

Evaluator   _____

✓ School-Aged Motor Skills Checklist

■ Section 1

Many items listed in this section are individual motor skills that do not depend on teammates or group recreational activities.

Compare the student to other children of the same age as you complete this checklist. Check each item the student **had trouble learning** or **is still unable to do**.

▶ Ball Skills •

❑ catches a large ball with two hands

❑ catches balls of differing sizes

❑ throws balls, beanbags, and rings into a specified target, using underhand action

❑ rolls or kicks balls toward an intended goal

❑ looks at a target, steps into the action, and then throws an object at the same time, such as a beanbag, a ring, or a ball

❑ judges target distance and matches it with the required force and action, not over-shooting the target or throwing the object too lightly

❑ uses an overhand action to throw a ball, a ring, or a beanbag

❑ strikes a ball or other object with a bat, a paddle, or a racquet

continued on next page

❏ tosses a ball back and forth with a partner, using a small ball and one or two hands for catching

❏ controls a soccer ball with proper foot action when running down a field

❏ bounces a basketball about 25 times in a row with control of force and direction

▶ Balance Activities ••

❏ extends both arms properly and independently for balance, such as while jumping on a trampoline or walking backward or forward on a narrow beam

❏ walks backward with confidence and control

❏ jumps off a small ledge without losing balance when landing

❏ takes a wide step or jumps over small objects on the ground, such as a branch or a row of bricks

❏ stands on tiptoes while walking in a specific pattern

❏ walks slowly without looking specifically at the floor, as when bringing someone a full glass of juice without spilling any of it

❏ stands on one leg while putting on a pair of pants, shorts, socks, or shoes

▶ Sports and Recreation ••

❏ climbs and hangs on monkey bars and other outdoor play equipment

❏ rides a three-wheeled bicycle or similar pedal toy without assistance

❏ runs fast and in a relatively straight line while looking backward and/or around at other items in the environment, as when trying to raise a kite into the sky to maintain a flying position

❏ walks, marches, dances, or in other ways keeps time with music

❏ maneuvers through, over, under, and around an obstacle course

❏ changes direction and speed while running, as when playing tag or other chasing games

continued on next page

❑ uses a jump rope alone or with friends

❑ plays floor or ice hockey by controlling the puck with a stick

❑ serves a volleyball over a net

❑ uses various racquets, bats, and clubs with reasonable control

❑ breathes rhythmically and systematically while swimming, as when doing a front crawl the width of a swimming pool

❑ hits a badminton birdie or a tennis ball over a net with control and strategy

❑ applies proper force during motor actions, such as when hitting a Ping-Pong ball with a paddle

❑ coordinates ball action by operating triggers and levers on a pinball machine

▶ **Personal Care and Hygiene** •

❑ displays excellent posture when walking or sitting

❑ fastens buttons and zippers on shirts, pants, jackets, and other clothing

❑ combs hair, brushes teeth, and washes hands and face

❑ squeezes toothpaste on a toothbrush and brushes teeth properly

❑ ties shoelaces

❑ fastens a belt buckle or other similar device

❑ puts a watch on independently

❑ manages all bathroom skills, including locking and unlocking an individual cubicle in a public building, manipulating clothes, wiping self, controlling the amount of toilet paper being used, and washing/drying hands at the sink

❑ trims own fingernails and toenails

❑ (for females) applies lipstick, mascara, and other make-up properly

❑ puts on earrings and fastens necklaces without using a mirror

continued on next page

▶ Household Tasks ••

❏ pushes large objects and furniture pieces around the home, such as a chair, a small table, or a large cardboard box

❏ uses a shovel or rake to perform outdoor work

❏ carries heavy bags or large boxes without close supervision

❏ turns doorknobs, dials, and faucets on and off with sufficient force

❏ uses and manipulates paper clips and safety pins properly

❏ manipulates and turns keys in door and car locks to open them

▶ Kitchen and Food Preparation ••••••••••••••••••••••••••••••••••••

❏ pours liquids from one container to another without excessive spillage

❏ unwraps candy and small items

❏ opens lids on bottles and small containers

❏ puts butter, jam, or other spreads on breads, as in making sandwiches

❏ manipulates a knife, fork, and spoon properly

❏ washes and dries dishes

❏ uses a manual can or bottle opener

❏ peels apples, potatoes, oranges, and other fruits and vegetables

❏ helps with cutting, dicing, slicing, and other types of food preparation in the kitchen

▶ Tabletop Activities ••

❏ picks up small objects from a counter or table, such as coins, buttons, or beads

❏ puts small items into a little hole or slot, such as placing pennies into a piggy bank or marbles into a small box or hole, as in a marble maze

continued on next page

❏ turns the pages of a book easily and quickly

❏ folds paper

❏ manipulates puzzle pieces, nails, or small pegs by turning or flipping them with one hand

❏ performs arts-and-crafts activities with proficiency

❏ holds and uses a paintbrush or felt marker with appropriate pressure

❏ independently strings beads onto a thread or a thin rope

❏ threads a needle

❏ uses wrapping paper and tape to wrap a present and then places a bow and greeting card on the top

❏ plans ahead and draws between narrow lines, as when following the correct track within a maze

❏ draws a person with at least eight different, distinguishable body parts

❏ shuffles and deals cards to several players

▶ **School Skills and Other Fine Motor Activities** •

❏ stays inside the lines when coloring

❏ traces pictures and performs other simple copying tasks

❏ uses scissors properly and cuts on straight and curved lines

❏ works well with stickers and glue to paste items onto paper

❏ draws simple geometric shapes and writes letters and numbers neatly and consistently

❏ forms letters between the lines and uses margins correctly on a sheet of paper

❏ plays a musical instrument

❏ types quickly and accurately on a computer keyboard or similar typing device

continued on next page

▶ Other Gross Motor Activities ••••••••••••••••••••••••••••••••••••••

- ❏ climbs up a ladder or a very steep set of stairs, as on a slide

- ❏ steps on and off objects of differing heights without using a handrail

- ❏ hops, leaps, skips, or gallops properly for a minimum of ten steps

- ❏ comprehends how to do – and then performs – a three-step action, such as a hop, then a step, then a jump

- ❏ follows simple directions properly in physical education class, such as doing push-ups and sit-ups when shown these skills

- ❏ plays hopscotch

- ❏ rides a two-wheeled bicycle without training wheels

- ❏ coordinates both sides of the body at the same time, as when doing jumping jacks

- ❏ walks or runs up and down stairs without looking at the steps or holding onto the handrails (may even extend stride to do two stairs at a time to go faster)

- ❏ understands and follows *right/left* directions quickly

■ Section 2

Check each item that applies to the student in the following areas.

▶ General Characteristics ••••••••••••••••••••••••••••••••••••••

- ❏ is generally delayed two or more years in developing motor skills

- ❏ displays poor ability with various sized balls in almost all throwing, kicking, catching, and striking actions

- ❏ performs culturally relevant motor skills at lower levels and with unacceptable proficiency, such as when in-line skating or riding a bicycle, scooter, or skateboard

- ❏ demonstrates a low level of physical fitness; lacks strength and endurance

continued on next page

The Source for DCD　　　　　65

❑ may be slightly overweight

❑ exhibits delay in performing motor tasks

❑ does not learn new motor skills quickly

❑ attempts specific motor activities a few times, but then stops soon after

❑ often has difficulty following a rhythm, such as tapping toes or fingers, clapping hands, and in other ways keeping time to music

❑ is socially isolated or has very few friends

▶ Limited Body Awareness •

❑ has limited general awareness of body/limb position, whether moving or still

❑ seems to stumble over his or her own feet; movements seem jerky or awkward

❑ moves awkwardly; displays stiff body action or too much rotation and excessive movement of other body parts

❑ able to perform one or more motor skills with some level of proficiency, but finds other motor tasks extremely challenging

❑ "freezes" while on a certain piece of equipment or has trouble initiating a motor task when others are watching

❑ is very anxious or shows signs of fear or intense resistance to becoming involved in a specific, novel motor activity, such as wall-climbing, navigating a ropes course, or going down a steep slide at a water park

❑ displays overflow movements during times of intense concentration, such as having an open mouth and moving the lips and/or tongue involuntarily when performing motor activities

❑ overestimates personal ability and, as a result, is unaware of the danger or risk involved in certain actions

❑ underestimates personal ability and does not even attempt a simple motor task because of being unsure of the goal, sequence, or speed with which to perform the skill

continued on next page

66

▶ Reduced Motivation to Participate in Active Events •

❑ displays reduced motivation to participate in any physical activity

❑ tends to avoid taking turns in sports-related activities

❑ excessively dislikes being involved in running and chasing games

❑ often withdraws from physical activities and associated environments; may lean against the school walls or sit alone during recess, lunch, and/or other school events. The student may not want to join in with the youth group activities at church, family functions, or other similar events in the neighborhood or larger community.

❑ is the last student to enter the gym for P.E. class

❑ often requests notes from home to be excused from P.E. or other recreational activities

❑ often resists entering novel settings involving physical activity, such as a new swimming pool. Once there, the student may hold onto the edge of the pool or rarely venture into deep water.

❑ tries to appear busy during P.E. or at a group event. Close observation reveals that the student is moving around, but not truly involved in the required tasks.

❑ complains of stomachaches and other ailments as a way to avoid physical activity

❑ does not initiate involvement in sports or want to be the first person to volunteer for physical demonstrations. Instead, the student prefers to wait and see what others do.

❑ follows other classmates or game players around but seldom actively engages in the game or recreational activity

❑ often avoids or is afraid of becoming involved in the center of action in a game situation; may act juvenile, such as closing her eyes and/or hiding behind her arms if a ball is thrown her way

continued on next page

▶ **Poor Motor Organization and Planning** •

❏ tends to have a poor understanding of the object of various games and activities; may score in the opposite team's goal, may not be sure when to chase someone, or may run in the wrong direction when being chased

❏ does not naturally step into a physical activity, such as taking a step before throwing a ball or serving in volleyball. If the student does take a step, the foot and arm action is incorrect.

❏ does not automatically bend knees slightly to get into the ready position when preparing to catch, jump, hop, or in other ways respond to sporting activities, such as when taking free throws in basketball

❏ has great difficulty with tasks that involve moving objects and individuals, or entire teams moving around them, such as basketball, football, or soccer. In such situations, the student may also have trouble remembering numerous rules at the same time.

❏ performs one component of a complex motor skill by isolating one body part and forgetting other coordinated movements

❏ misjudges distances and speed; "timing" is frequently inaccurate. The student has great difficulty entering or leaving changing environments, such as a turning jump rope, a moving merry-go-round, or a moving swing or similar object.

❏ has difficulty focusing on the important components of a motor skill demonstration; may be unsure what to look at when watching someone perform a lay-up in basketball, execute the preliminary action involved in discus throw, etc.

❏ prefers involvement in individual motor skills that have repetitive components to them, such as swimming, dance, or bicycling

continued on next page

► Penmanship ··

- ❏ uses excessive pressure when writing or drawing

- ❏ complains of a very sore hand after writing for a period of time. The student may actually shake the hand to get some relief.

- ❏ sometimes holds the head at an awkward tilt or in an unusual manner when doing fine motor skills at a table or desk

- ❏ often holds items very close to the eyes or positions the head very close to the desk when writing or drawing

- ❏ exaggerates finger movements during various fine motor tasks. For example, when using the index finger and thumb to pick up tacks, straight pins, or coins from a table, the child holds the other fingers in an extended or stiff position.

► Resistant Attitude

- ❏ gives up very quickly; lacks persistence and seems easily frustrated

- ❏ claims to have "forgotten" gym clothes, swimsuit, or other items and equipment for physical activity

- ❏ easily becomes upset and exhibits difficulty with failure

- ❏ displays challenging behaviors by withdrawing, refusing to participate, clowning around, disturbing other students, and/or showing frustration by crying, stomping, and stating that the activity is "stupid." These behaviors often serve as avoidance strategies for the student with motor problems.

■ Checklist Summary

If you have marked most of the examples on this entire checklist as being problematic, you should consider scheduling the student for a check-up as soon as possible, including vision and hearing testing. Consider whether the items you have checked are mostly gross motor skills, mostly fine motor skills, or a combination. This information will be very important for your medical professional.

Chapter Two

■ Summary

Parents who have children with speech, social, or motor difficulties are often referred by doctors to meet with other professionals during their child's formative years. Since speech is an oral-motor control skill, and research has shown that many children who have difficulties with oral language production also have other motor problems, an SLP will likely meet and work with these youngsters at some point in time. Most of these clinicians have excellent observation skills and would likely spot a child who has some other motor issues.

One way an SLP can identify children with additional motor concerns is by noting how slowly and awkwardly the child moves and by analyzing how much additional help the child requires to perform the various activities required in therapy sessions. It is critical for any professional who works with very young children to make all concerns known to parents so that identification and intervention for the child can start as soon as possible.

The example of Marco's difficulties before and during his school years demonstrated the urgency for early identification and support. His story showed how debilitating a lack of motor skill development and learning can be. This example led into a discussion about the relationship of motor difficulties and how they impact psychosocial development. Numerous studies have shown that children who struggle with learning and performing motor skills tend to withdraw and isolate themselves from their peers. This behavior begins a vicious cycle that can eventually lead to sadness, depression, anxiety, and other serious mental heath concerns. An inactive lifestyle can also result in problems with physical health. The *competence motivation theory* explains the relationship between difficulties in the motor domain and the resultant mental health concerns.

The final section of the chapter provided checklists of different motor skills that parents, caregivers, and other adults can use to evaluate a child. The checklists are geared for preschool children and elementary students and preadolescent/adolescent students. The activities on these checklists relate to physical activities performed at home or school. Having more than one adult complete a checklist for a given student helps parents and professionals gain an objective perspective of the student's motor abilities and determine whether referral to a specialist is warranted.

Chapter Two

Most of the information in this chapter described the types of fine and gross motor activities usually performed at home and/or in school. Unfortunately, because children do not grow out of their motor difficulties when they graduate from school, and as part of learning about potential problems in adulthood, in the next chapter, you will read how motor skill difficulties may relate to the adult workplace.

Chapter Two

References

- Bruininks, R.H. (1978). *Bruininks-Oseretsky test of motor proficiency.* Circle Pines, MN: American Guidance Service.

- Causgrove-Dunn, J., & Watkinson, E.J. (1994). A study of the relationship between physical awkwardness and children's perceptions of physical competence. *Adapted Physical Activity Quarterly, 11*, 274-283.

- Causgrove-Dunn, J., & Watkinson, E.J. (2002). Considering motivation theory in the study of developmental coordination disorder. In S.A. Chermak & D. Larkin (Eds.), *Developmental Coordination Disorder* (pp. 185-199). Clifton Park, NY: Thompson Delmar Learning.

- Estil, L.B., & Whiting, H.T.A. (2002). Motor/language impairment syndromes: Direct or indirect foundations. In S.A. Chermak & D. Larkin (Eds.), *Developmental Coordination Disorder* (pp. 54-68). Clifton Park, NY: Thompson Delmar Learning.

- Folio, M.R., & Fewell, R.R. (1983). *Peabody developmental motor scales and activity cards.* Austin, TX: PRO-ED.

- Frankenburg, W.K., & Dodds, J.B. (1967). *The Denver developmental screening test.* Denver, CO: University of Colorado Medical Center.

- Hay, J., & Missiuna, C. (1998). Motor proficiency in children reporting low levels of participation in physical activity. *Canadian Journal of Occupational Therapy, 65*(2), 64-71.

- Henderson, S.E., & Sugden, D.A. (1992). *Movement assessment battery for children.* London: The Psychological Corporation, Ltd.

- Kamps, P.H. (2004). Developmental coordination disorder. *Advance for Speech-Language Pathologists and Audiologists, 14,* 12.

- Le Normand, M.T., Vaivre-Douret, L., Payan, C., & Cohen, H. (2000). Neuromotor development and language processing in developmental dyspraxia: A follow-up case study. *Journal of Clinical and Experimental Neuropsychology, (22)*3, 408-417.

Chapter Two

• McCabe, P., Rosenthal, J.B., & McLeod, S. (1998). Features of developmental dyspraxia in the general speech-impaired population. *Clinical Linguistics & Phonetics, 12*(2), 105.

• Missiuna, C. (1998). Development of "All About Me," a scale that measures children's perceived motor competence. *The Occupational Therapy Journal of Research, 18*(2), 85-108.

• Missiuna, C., Gaines, B.R., & Pollock, N. (2002). Recognizing and referring children at risk for developmental coordination disorder: Role of speech language pathologist. *Journal of Speech-Language Pathology and Audiology, (26)*4, 170-177.

• Schoemaker, M.M., & Kalverboer, A.F. (1994). Social and affective problems of children who are clumsy: How early do they begin? *Adapted Physical Activity Quarterly, 11*, 130-140.

• Skinner, R.A., & Piek, J.P. (1994). Psychosocial implications of poor motor coordination in children and adolescents. In P.J. Beek & P.C.W. van Wieringen (Eds.), *Human Movement Science, 20,* 73-94.

• Stott, D.H., Moyes, F.A., & Henderson, S.E. (1972). *Test of motor impairment.* Guelph, ON, Canada: Brook Educational.

• Wessel, J.A. (1976). *I CAN fundamental skills.* Austin, TX: PRO-ED.

Chapter Three

This chapter presents information about four topics:

1 Case Studies

Two case studies will demonstrate the importance of an accurate, timely diagnosis of motor difficulties. They will also show how even trained professionals can miss the impact and real cause of the motor difficulties.

2 A Quick Lesson About Intelligence Testing

In order to assist with the diagnosis of DCD and other specific disorders, there is an expectation that the clinician has measured the individual's intellectual ability. Therefore, this chapter will also include a section on cognitive testing and what certain numbers and terms mean.

3 Description and Diagnosis of DCD

This section presents the description and diagnostic features of DCD and discusses its diagnosis.

4 Other Conditions That Affect Motor Coordination

In addition to DCD, some of the other related disorders that impact motor skill development and performance will be identified and discussed. They will be compared with and contrasted to DCD.

■ Case Studies

The following case studies are based on psychological testing and refer to measured cognitive abilities. Even if you are not clear about psychological or cognitive assessment, do read the case studies. Then later in the chapter, after the reading about cognitive testing and what some of the relevant terms mean, you may want to reread each case study. This rereading will increase your understanding of the concepts you just learned about, and specific terms and values will likely become much more meaningful to you.

► **Case Study One**

*E**than** is a fifth-grade student who attends a community public school in a large metropolitan center in North America. Ethan was referred for a psycho-educational assessment to investigate what could be causing his difficulties with academic and fine motor skill performance. His parents also wanted to know what types of strategies would help him succeed in school.*

Ethan is the oldest child of Scott and DeAnne, both highly-educated people who are employed as an engineer and a nurse respectively. Ethan has one six-year-old sister named Elena. About five years ago, the family moved to this city as a result of a job transfer for the father. They do not have any immediate or extended family in this city, but they have developed a supportive circle of friends and acquaintances.

Ethan's parents report that he is a polite, honest, respectful boy who has a very good nature. He is well behaved and has a good sense of humor. He is a very strong athlete and enjoys participating in many sports, such as soccer, baseball, and hockey. Ethan also enjoys riding his bicycle and skateboard. Areas that are problematic for him include any task involving written communication and other fine motor skills. As a result of some of these motor difficulties, Ethan experiences difficulty in language arts, social studies, science, and math.

Ethan's parents first became concerned about his fine motor difficulties when he was in kindergarten, yet the first time that teachers informed the parents of any academic concerns occurred when Ethan was in second grade. As a result of this concern, Ethan was assessed by a local school psychologist. Using the WISC-III, the psychologist reported that Ethan's Full Scale cognitive score fell in the borderline range (5th percentile) and that his Verbal and Performance scale scores were at the 5th and 10th percentiles (borderline and low-average ranges respectively). She also reported that Ethan fell in the intellectually deficient range for Freedom from Distractibility and the borderline range for Processing Speed. Additional testing in reading, writing, and math showed that Ethan was barely managing current grade expectations, but his scores were somewhat consistent with his low cognitive scores.

Because of the reported fine motor concerns, the psychologist also administered the Beery VMI *and the supplemental* VMI *tests. Ethan scored in the average range for all three tests: Visual-Motor Skills, Motor Coordination Skills, and Visual Acuity (23rd, 18th, and 14th percentiles respectively). The psychologist noted that Ethan experienced qualitative difficulties with fine motor tasks such as printing, but she did not identify any type of learning disability. Rather, she felt that Ethan was a slow learner who was working at academic levels that were slightly above his measured cognitive ability.*

Since Ethan was also having behavioral difficulties at school, the psychologist asked his teacher and parents to rate Ethan's behaviors on the Behavior Assessment System for Children (BASC). *When results were tallied and analyzed, Ethan was reported to have features of aggression, depression, attention, and learning problems. However, these were not reported as being clinically significant. No other assessment was conducted, no diagnosis was made, and Ethan remained in his regular second-grade class with no formal support.*

All the same, because of Ethan's ongoing problems with printing, he was referred for occupational therapy (OT) assistance at school. A few months later, the parents heard about and enrolled their son in a summer OT program. His legibility, consistency of letter formation, placement of letters on the paper, and rate of work were addressed in the three-week program. After the course of treatment, he had made minimal gains in basic printing skills, yet the OT noted ongoing difficulties with manual dexterity, fine motor control, visual-motor planning, and coordination. More visits, instructional sessions, and consultations by the OT were continued until Ethan was discharged in June 2003 (the end of third grade).

> After the course of treatment, he had made minimal gains in basic printing skills, yet the OT noted ongoing difficulties with manual dexterity, fine motor control, visual-motor planning, and coordination.

76

Chapter Three

Three years later, Ethan still struggles with completing most writing tasks at school and home. His parents also report that he has ongoing problems with printing and/or cursive writing and even basic coloring tasks. He also continues to have difficulties using scissors and other tools properly (e.g., knife and fork). Nevertheless, Ethan's parents and teachers report that he displays an excellent attitude toward learning and that he works very hard at school. Once again, the parents sought help for the cause of their son's fine motor problems. Via a referral by friends, they contacted this psychologist.

During an extensive family interview, I asked many questions about Ethan's health, medical conditions, and other physical factors. DeAnne reported that her pregnancy and Ethan's birth were rather uneventful. Ethan was a healthy, full-term baby who acquired motor milestones within typical time frames. However, his speech was somewhat delayed and Ethan began stuttering at about age three. DeAnne felt that Ethan had age-appropriate language skills in most other areas (e.g., vocabulary development, receptive language, and creating and retelling stores). An SLP assessed Ethan and diagnosed moderate levels of stuttering and some "weakness in concept development in the areas of school readiness." To address this, Ethan participated in speech therapy from the time he was four years old until he was eight, by which time his dysfluent speech was corrected.

Ethan's hearing was tested when in ECS and found to be in the normal range. His vision was assessed about one year before meeting the new examiner and no concerns were evident. He had also been tested for allergies and, although he had had reactions to milk as an infant, no apparent allergies were present at time of the new psycho-educational testing. The areas of rest, relaxation, and nutrition were all assumed to be normal as he appeared very healthy and no other medical concerns were reported.

In addition to the speech/language and occupational therapy assessments and interventions, Ethan's parents reported that their son had also participated in an early literacy support program at his local school for the last four years. Because of Ethan's ongoing difficulties with writing, the school had already made allowances for him to have access to a computer in hopes that it would lessen the challenging printing and writing tasks required so frequently in school.

Chapter Three

Ethan's parents also provided the examiner with extensive school records, reports, and other related documents. There had been a very clear pattern of fine motor and speech difficulties throughout his early elementary years. Finally, when asked about family history, Scott and DeAnne reported that no other family members or relatives had similar problems in school. Ethan's parents were very curious to find out what was causing his difficulties.

When I had the privilege of meeting Ethan for the first time, he was just over ten years old. He presented as an attractive, healthy boy who seemed slightly shy at the beginning of the first assessment session. He was very polite and, over time, seemed to become more comfortable with the testing process.

Ethan made many interesting facial expressions and tended to frown when tasks became difficult. However, he showed a willingness to take risks and he also displayed remarkable persistence when questions were very hard. Ethan's response style could be described as somewhat slow and steady. He also appeared to have some word-finding problems. Ethan displayed good eye contact and asked for clarification when uncertain of the expectations of a task. During several paper/pencil tasks, he displayed a good tripod grip, but showed extensive overflow movements of the mouth (e.g., pursing and/or opening his lips, involuntary movement of his tongue). He also used excessive pencil pressure and worked slowly. These qualitative observations suggested that he was exerting significant cognitive energy while producing the fine motor actions, yet in general, Ethan was willing to do all tasks. His high level of cooperation and motivation seem to indicate that the following results were a reliable measure of his abilities.

Numerous assessment techniques, procedures, and tests were administered, including some standardized tests, some nonstandardized rating scales, as well as some qualitative measures. A review of the testing results is given on page 79.

Chapter Three

WISC-IV			
Factors	Index	95% Confidence Interval	Range
Verbal Comprehension	93	88-97	Average
Perceptual Reasoning	98	91-106	Average
Working Memory	107	99-114	Average
Processing Speed	85	78-96	Low Average
Full Scale	94	89-99	Average

From this table, one can see that the only area of relative weakness was Processing Speed (low average range). It is interesting to note that subtests assessing this factor are timed and involve paper/pencil tasks.

As mentioned earlier, the examiner noted that Ethan displayed overflow movements of the mouth only during the paper/pencil tasks. During such tasks, he produced individual letters rather quickly, forming his letters in unique ways, and his printed work revealed many spatial difficulties (e.g., letters in words were crowded, at times there were large spaces between words, some "tall letters" were the same size as "small letters," and many letters were positioned above the lines). He used margins correctly. Ethan made numerous spelling errors and wrote different letter forms for the same letter.

When given seven minutes and a picture prompt to write a short story, Ethan produced a logical, handwritten product that contained some details. However, he used very few descriptors and the three sentences he produced were not grammatically correct. Given the same amount of time to dictate a story to a scribe, Ethan's story was significantly longer and more descriptive, his grammar was appropriate, and his vocabulary usage was much enhanced.

To further assess his fine motor skills, Ethan was asked to participate in several activities of daily living. Although he performed most skills with a reasonable level of proficiency, there was an element of awkwardness about his movements and his performances were very slow. He also seemed to have tremendous difficulty with tasks involving buttons and using tools (e.g., pencil, knife and fork). In other assessment tasks, Ethan displayed a lack of planning and organization when drawing. He exhibited stronger skills in an oral vs. written spelling test and showed age-appropriate bilateral coordination and upper limb coordination.

The examiner also observed that Ethan had significant difficulty with rather simple fine motor tasks, especially when he was unable to use his eyes to track his finger movements. When further assessment of manual dexterity was conducted, Ethan scored below the 5th percentile on a standardized assessment. He continued to have great difficulty when required to manipulate fine motor objects quickly and accurately and when drawing specific designs with control and fluency. Once again, he displayed some overflow movements while performing these tasks.

When compared to other students the same age, Ethan has significant motor difficulties with manual dexterity.

Finally, Ethan's mom was asked to rate her son's abilities in numerous motor tasks. Although Ethan has well developed gross motor planning, control during movement, and general coordination, his mother's ratings indicated that her son has many problems with fine motor control.

In summary, Ethan's results in the cognitive domain fell within the average range, but he experienced many difficulties in activities of daily living and other fine motor skills required at school. A phone consultation with Dr. Tyless, Ethan's medical doctor, confirmed that there was no medical or neurological basis to his fine motor difficulties. Based on observations of Ethan, file review, interviews with Ethan's parents, assessment results, clinical judgment, and a review of the criteria in the DSM-VI-TR, Ethan was deemed to meet the diagnostic criteria of developmental coordination disorder (DCD). In addition, he met the criteria of a learning disability in written expression.

Overall, these findings and scores were significantly different from similar testing conducted three years ago when Ethan scored in the low-average, borderline, and intellectually deficient ranges on the

80

Chapter Three

cognitive assessment. It may be that Ethan was still somewhat shy or embarrassed about his weak verbal skills and did not want to express his knowledge because of his dysfluent speech at that time. In addition, because of his fine motor difficulties, his proficiency and speed in completing visual-spatial tasks was also likely much slower. If these factors were indeed present and impacting his performance during the original cognitive testing, as it seems they were, his resultant scores would (and did) fall in a much lower range.

Obviously Ethan is not a student of low cognitive ability, yet his weak motor skills in multiple areas created an impression that he was less capable than most of his peers. Fortunately, with parental support, early and ongoing intervention with SLP and OT, and accommodations at school, it appears that Ethan has developed some self-confidence about his abilities and is now much more willing (and able) to tell and display to others what he knows. Hence we now have a much more accurate portrayal of his skills and abilities and, maybe even more importantly, answers to parental questions about what is causing his difficulties at school!

▶ Case Study Two

Latisha is an eighth-grade student who lives with her parents and two younger brothers. She attends a local middle school in a city of about 60,000 people. Once again, her name has come forward for review with teachers, support staff, the principal, and her parents because of her poor attitude to learning, her weak academic performance, and her overall behavioral difficulties.

Latisha has been tested several times already. As early as first grade, her teachers put her name forward because of significant difficulties with task completion and attention. She was also thought to be excessively active (e.g., wiggly, fidgety, squirmy). The WISC-III, an achievement test, a classroom observation, and a checklist assessing the presence of AD/HD type behaviors were administered. A brief summary of her initial testing is presented on page 82.

Chapter Three

WISC-III

Factors	Index	95% Confidence Interval	Range
Verbal Comprehension	105	97-112	Average
Perceptual Reasoning	103	94-112	Average
Full Scale	104	97-111	Average

Achievement: K-TEA

Subtests	Index	95% Confidence Interval	Range
Mathematics	96	85-107	Average
Reading	101	91-111	Average
Spelling	107	96-118	Average

The examiner reported that overall, Latisha was functioning below her age and grade levels based on her measured level of cognitive functioning. Although the examiner noted that she had difficulty with fine motor skills and dexterity, her spelling skills still fell in the average range. The examiner attributed her printing and fine motor difficulties to her overactive classroom behaviors. The results of this testing were analyzed and the examiner concluded that Latisha was a young girl with average cognitive abilities who was not learning disabled – just underachieving in first grade already!

During a classroom observation, the examiner felt that Latisha displayed many off-task behaviors and noted that the teacher had to redirect her three times more often than her peers. As part of this initial evaluation, the teacher was asked to rate Latisha's behaviors on a form measuring AD/HD symptoms. Using T-score values in which any score above 70 is thought to fall in the clinically significant range, the teacher reported that Latisha displayed the following behaviors.

AD / HD Behaviors	T-Scores	Range
Opposition / Conduct Problems	100	Clinically Significant
Hyperactivity	99	Clinically Significant
Inattentiveness	75	Clinically Significant
Overall AD / HD Symptoms	101	Clinically Significant

Chapter Three

Although the psychologist indicated that Latisha had been very coop-erative and well behaved during the entire assessment session, the same examiner diagnosed her as having a severe "conduct problem" and suggested counseling for her behavioral difficulties. He also rec-ommended continued practice of printing because of her weak quality of pencil control. She was also encouraged to begin a comprehensive in-home reading program and placed on a behavior management system whereby her actions were monitored very closely. All of this occurred within the first seven months of first grade.

Latisha was assessed again when she was in fifth grade. By this time she was involved in a community-based program that dealt with students with mental health issues; she was struggling with anxiety and depression. Her social worker had requested an update on her skills and abilities. Latisha was retested by the same examiner, and her eventual cognitive scores differed from the initial results. They are presented below for your review.

WISC-III

Factors	Index	95% Confidence Interval	Range
Verbal Comprehension	99	92-106	Average
Perceptual Reasoning	119	110-128	Above Average
Full Scale	109	103-115	Average

Achievement: K-TEA

Subtests	Index	95% Confidence Interval	Range
Mathematics	105	95-116	Average
Reading	108	100-116	Average
Spelling	90	81-99	Average

Her fifth-grade teacher was asked to rate Latisha's classroom behav-iors. These results are presented on page 84.

AD / HD Behaviors	T-Scores	Range
Opposition / Conduct Problems	91	Clinically Significant
Hyperactivity	88	Clinically Significant
Inattentiveness	65	At-Risk
Overall AD / HD Symptoms	89	Clinically Significant

Once again, this child was not diagnosed as having any learning problems. Rather, the psychologist reported that the child displayed numerous outbursts and was defiant and unpredictable in class. In addition, the psychologist felt that her behaviors could be described as "oppositional and hyperactive." The primary recommendations were more counseling and the development of a structured behavior management plan.

Latisha moved on to middle school. Her sixth-grade teacher could not understand why this girl did not have an identifiable learning disability, so another assessment was conducted. This time, a different school psychologist asked Latisha to participate in a structured subtest measuring her writing skills. Latisha was resistant and required a great deal of prompting; however, she eventually wrote two sentences within the 15-minute time frame. Her sentences were disorganized and poorly developed. Her writing was very messy, she had many spelling errors, and she even seemed to have difficulty keeping her words between the margins and lines on the paper. Her sentence structure and use of grammar was appropriate. Latisha's score was found to fall in the low-average range, and finally, she was recognized as having a learning disability. Her programming expectations and writing assignments were altered, and she was allowed to have a scribe for examinations.

Later Latisha was assessed again for problematic behavior at school. Using the BASC, her teacher indicated that she had very weak study and social skills, elevated levels of anxiety, hyperactivity, aggression, and clinically significant scores for depression and somatization. On a more detailed depression inventory, Latisha reported that she felt incompetent in school, had difficulty sleeping and eating, and lacked "fun." Latisha often felt very sad and her score on self-esteem was highly negative. She admitted that she was very unhappy, had nightmares, and did not feel connected to her peers. Because of her apparent state of depression, the psychologist referred the family to a community-based mental health program. Latisha's parents were encouraged to enroll her into various programs and counseling sessions within this program.

During seventh grade, Latisha continued to struggle to complete classroom assignments and other projects. Even after her mother explained to the staff that it took her several hours to do a rather simple project, such as cut out pictures from a magazine and glue them on a poster board, Latisha was still expected to perform the same assignments as her classmates. It wasn't many months after this that other major decisions were made on this student's behalf. Although her parents were resistant, the school admitted that they were unable to meet her educational needs. As such, this young teen was sent to a special school for students with major emotional problems. It is quite probable that she will spend several years in this setting. The decision to transfer her was facilitated by all the reports and recommendations made since her very first years in school. Tragically, Latisha had struggled with undiagnosed DCD. Her problems with writing and fine motor skills were improperly labeled as "behavior issues." Although she was in "treatment," the underlying issues were not correctly identified or dealt with.

Very clearly, motor skill difficulties impact other aspects of life.

■ A Quick Lesson About Intelligence Testing

Since several of the *DSM-IV-TR* diagnostic terms that will be explained in this book refer to *measured intelligence*, it is important that you have some understanding of this term, as well as how scores are identified and how they are distributed in the general population.

The term *intelligence* generally refers to thinking and reasoning skills and the recall and overall understanding that one has and uses throughout the life span. There are multiple definitions of *intelligence* and to list them all would fill up many pages in this book. In general, *intelligence* is a word that is used to indicate one's quality of reasoning. Intelligence involves the ability to acquire, store, and retrieve information effectively, as when required to recall and use background knowledge and past experiences in novel ways when solving problems. Intelligence also involves the ability to learn, adapt to circumstances, or reach a desired end in a creative or efficient manner, all the while taking cultural values into account. Intelligence is a quality

Chapter Three

that allows one to think rationally and to maintain and pursue conceptual skills and abilities, even when this requires one to utilize excessive concentration and energy while withstanding emotional extremes.

The *Merriam-Webster Online* dictionary definition states that intelligence is the ability to "learn or understand or to deal with new or trying situations; the skilled use of reason; the ability to apply knowledge to manipulate one's environment or to think abstractly as measured by objective criteria (as tests)" (*www.m-w.com*, 2005).

This definition has changed over the years. According to online data, in 1913, Webster's definition of intelligence was "the act or state of knowing; the exercise of the understanding; the capacity to know or understand; readiness of comprehension."

Intelligence impacts one's ability to process information.

For the purposes of this book, and stated much more simply, intelligence impacts one's ability to process information. For example, the amount of intelligence one has affects the individual's ability to learn, solve problems, recognize patterns, perform tasks quickly and efficiently, comprehend information, and determine what environmental stimuli is important and worth monitoring vs. what information is irrelevant and should be screened out.

Research reveals that each of us is born with a particular amount of cognitive ability and, for the most part, this amount tends to be stable over time. Our cognitive ability is genetically determined and contributed by our parents at conception. However, some studies have shown that intelligence can be altered somewhat, based on environmental conditions. For example, if you have a stable home life; proper nutrition and medical care; enriched educational opportunities; and many opportunities to listen, watch, and in other ways learn from your educated parents, neighbors, and family friends, you will likely exhibit a higher intelligence score than someone who did not have these opportunities.

Although there is much debate in the literature about different types of intelligence and how to measure it, such discussions are far too complex and detailed for inclusion in this resource. Those topics have been the subject of numerous research studies and many books, articles, and journals for decades. For the purposes of this book, you need to know that intelligence is measured using standardized tests and that results are reported as IQ scores.

Chapter Three

IQ refers to one's *intelligence quotient*. To determine this quotient, a child's measured mental age is divided by the child's chronological age (how many days, months, and years old the child is).

Chronological age is easy to calculate because we use a standard system to mark the passage of time. For example, let's say a young boy named Matthew just had his tenth birthday last week. His chronological age would be 10 years, 0 months, and 7 days.

In contrast, one's mental age is measured through very specialized testing that must be done the exact same way on every person who is tested. This testing method is called *standardized testing*. There are very specific standards one must follow when conducting a cognitive assessment, such as who is permitted to conduct the testing, how the test is administered, how much time is permitted to answer questions, what answer constitutes a correct response, etc.

Suppose Matthew, at age 10, scored a mental age of 12 during standardized testing. Dividing his mental age (12) by his chronological age (10), Matthew would earn a quotient of 1.2.

Step One:

$$\frac{12 \text{ (Matthew' scored mental age)}}{10 \text{ (Matthew's chronological age)}} = 1.2$$

This quotient is then multiplied by 100 to determine the actual intelligence quotient, which would be 120 in this case. Since IQ scores are distributed on a continuum with 100 as its middle value, Matthew would have an IQ of 120, which is above the average range.

Step Two:

1.2 multiplied by 100 = 120 (Matthew's measured intelligence quotient)

Meaning:

An IQ score of 120 is considered relatively high. Most parents would be thrilled to know that their child has an IQ of 120. It means that although Matthew is only 10 years old, his cognitive functioning reflects someone who is 12 years of age. In summary, Matthew's cognitive skills appear to be advanced beyond that of most other students his same age.

If a 10-year-old boy named Takashi had a mental age score of 10 years, his measured IQ would be 100.

Step One:

$$\frac{10 \text{ (Takashi's scored mental age)}}{10 \text{ (Takashi's chronological age)}} = 1.0$$

Step Two:

1.0 multiplied by 100 = 100 (Takashi's measured intelligence quotient)

Meaning:

In this case, the IQ score of 100 means that Takashi's cognitive skills appear to be exactly what one would expect. He is functioning at a level that is consistent with most other 10-year-old children.

Test developers record results on a bell-shaped curve to indicate the variance within the general population (for intelligence or any other measured factor). This means that, for any feature measured, most people's results would fall somewhere in the middle. For a fictitious example, if 100 randomly selected adult women in North America were measured for height, most scores would likely fall somewhere between 5'1" and 5'8" (or 155–174 centimeters). The women whose height fell between 5'1"–5'8" would be considered average in height. Shorter women would be positioned below the average designation while women taller than 5'8" would be above the average range. The same rules would apply if one measured the weight of 100 people.

To help researchers, clinicians, and other people make meaning of and be able to compare IQ scores among people and compare values over time, specific terms have been designated to indicate the range a person falls into (e.g., *high average*, *low average*, *average*). Statisticians have also assigned standard scores and percentiles to match specific values in these ranges.

When explaining how cognitive ability is measured, the following is true for most intelligence tests. Because of the general variance in population, 10 points in either direction of the midpoint standard score, 100, indicates a different category of cognitive ability. For example, the range between 90-100 and 100-109 is the average or normal range. Do you recall our 10-year-old-boy named Takashi? He scored the same as other peers the exact same age. His standard score was 100. That means his score was exactly in the middle of where most other 10-year-olds also score. This standard score of 100 also equates to the 50th percentile. On each side of this normal range is a 10-point section that also represents scores in the average range. Nevertheless, scores from 80 to 89 are low average while scores from 110 to 119 are high average. Children who score between 120 and 129 are classified within the superior range, and those at or above 130 are considered to be gifted and have a very superior intelligence.

Bell-shaped Curve

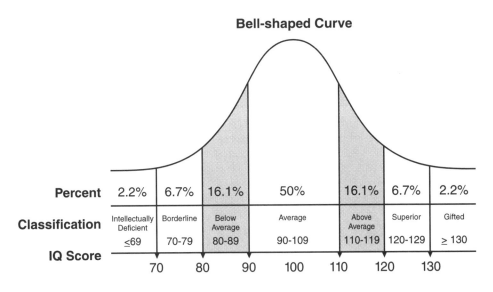

Percent	2.2%	6.7%	16.1%	50%	16.1%	6.7%	2.2%
Classification	Intellectually Deficient	Borderline	Below Average	Average	Above Average	Superior	Gifted
	≤69	70-79	80-89	90-109	110-119	120-129	≥ 130
IQ Score	70	80	90	100	110	120	130

Although many parents desire to have their child's IQ score far above 100, the reality is that only half of the population obtains IQ scores at and above 100. That means that the remainder of the population has scores below 100. Students who score less than the low-average range are considered to fall in the borderline range (from 70 to 79 on intelligence tests). If IQ scores fall below 69, and other testing results verify these low values, the student may receive a diagnosis of intellectual deficiency, mental retardation (MR), or some other diagnosis, such as pervasive developmental disorder (PDD). These terms and disorders will be discussed later in the chapter.

In order to have the official diagnosis of mental retardation, intellectual deficiency, or cognitive delay, there must be consistency of scores between a cognitive assessment (intelligence test) and equally low scores on an assessment that measures adaptive functioning (how well a person can perform various skills independently). This strategy ensures that the child did not have exceptionally poor performance (or heightened anxiety) on the day of the intelligence testing. Although it does not happen frequently, it is possible for students to score low on a cognitive assessment but have age-appropriate skills in many other areas (self-help, community self-sufficiency, personal development, etc.).

The reason it is important to present the information about intelligence scores at this time in the book is that the next few topics refer to individuals with average to above-average intelligence. While this typically includes students who have an IQ score of 90 or higher on an intelligence test, an argument can be made to include those in the below-average category as well, especially if the clinician feels the testing results may be an underestimate of the student's skills and abilities.

In short, when a child participates in an intelligence test, it is likely that he or she will score within the average range. (Note: The intelligence quotient or IQ is also known as the *standard score* or *index* and will probably fall between 90 and 109 for half of the population. You can see in the diagram on page 89 that 50% of the population who participate in intelligence tests have a score that falls within this average group.) Those who score lower than the average range are said to display cognitive skills that are slightly younger or more delayed than their chronological ages, while those who score higher than 109 are said to have cognitive functioning that is more advanced than one would expect for their chronological ages.

■ Description and Diagnosis of DCD

▶ Description

Numerous conditions affect the acquisition and performance of gross motor skills, such as cerebral palsy, hemiplegia, or muscular dystrophy. This section offers detailed information about developmental coordination disorder (DCD), a lesser-known condition that can also affect fine and gross motor skills. For most of the disorders described in this book, the diagnostic information and terms identified in the *Diagnostic and Statistical Manual - Fourth Edition - Text Revision (DSM-IV-TR)* will be used because this is the most recent resource available to healthcare professionals for making a diagnosis.

The *DSM-IV-TR* is a manual that psychiatrists, medical doctors, and chartered psychologists use when they make a diagnosis. This resource describes many different disorders, and all of the conditions are said to impact psychosocial development or social-emotional functioning in some way; that is why they are included in that manual. Some of the conditions documented in the *DSM-IV-TR* relate primarily to children under 18 years of age while others are specifically geared to the making of a diagnosis for adults. A few *DSM-IV-TR* common diagnostic terms you may already know or have heard before include such terms as *mental retardation, pervasive developmental disorder (PDD), bipolar disorder, schizophrenia, learning disabilities*, and *attention deficit/hyperactivity disorder (AD/HD)*. Over time, these conditions can affect the psychosocial or emotional realms.

Developmental coordination disorder (DCD) is a clearly defined condition that is described in the *DSM-IV-TR*. DCD is the only condition featured in the section "Motor Skills Disorder." In short, the diagnostic term *DCD* is used to identify children less than 18 years of age who, although they score in the average to above-average range of intelligence (or higher), are significantly delayed in the development, acquisition, and performance of motor skills. It is sometimes referred to as a "motor learning disability." For the most part, children with DCD have great difficulty coordinating voluntary movements (physical activity they want to do). Voluntary motor activity is different from moving as a result of reflex activity, which is also known as *involuntary movement*. Motor difficulties can be evident in only fine motor skills, in only gross motor activities, or in both fine and gross motor skills. Furthermore, research shows that DCD can affect oral motor and other motor functioning mentioned earlier in this book. The resulting challenges usually create problems at home and/or at school. Research involving students with DCD shows that the motor difficulty also impacts other domains of behavior.

▶ Diagnostic Features

The information in the box on page 92 is reprinted with permission from the *Diagnostic and Statistical Manual of Mental Disorders, Text Revision*, Copyright 2000, American Psychiatric Association. In summary, a diagnosis of DCD can be made if the following four criteria are met:

1 Criterion A

Performance in daily activities that require motor coordination is substantially below that expected given the person's chronological age and measured intelligence. This may be manifested by marked delays in achieving motor milestones – walking, crawling, sitting, dropping things, clumsiness, poor performance in sports, or poor handwriting (p. 58).[1]

---

[1] Reprinted with permission from the *Diagnostic and Statistical Manual of Mental Disorders, Text Revision*, Copyright 2000. American Psychiatric Association.

Chapter Three

315.4 Developmental Coordination Disorder

■ Diagnostic Features

The essential feature of Developmental Coordination Disorder is a marked impairment in the development of motor coordination (Criterion A). The diagnosis is made only if this impairment significantly interferes with academic achievement or activities of daily living (Criterion B). The diagnosis is made if the coordination difficulties are not due to a general medical condition (e.g., cerebral palsy, hemiplegia, or muscular dystrophy) and the criteria are not met for Pervasive Developmental Disorder (Criterion C). If Mental Retardation (MR) is present, the motor difficulties are in excess of those usually associated with it (Criterion D). The manifestations of this disorder vary with age and development. For example, younger children may display clumsiness and delays in achieving developmental milestones, such as walking, crawling, sitting, tying shoelaces, buttoning shirts, and zipping pants. Older children may display difficulties with the motor aspects of assembling puzzles, building models, playing ball, and printing or handwriting.

■ Associated Features and Disorders

Problems commonly associated with Developmental Coordination Disorder include delays in other non-motor milestones. Associated disorders may include Phonological Disorder, Expressive Language Disorder, and Mixed Receptive-Expressive Language Disorder.

■ Prevalence

Prevalence of Developmental Coordination Disorder has been estimated to be as high as 6% for children in the age range of 5-11 years.

■ Course

Recognition of Developmental Coordination Disorder usually occurs when the child first attempts tasks such as running, holding a knife and fork, buttoning clothes, or playing ball games. The course is variable. In some cases, lack of coordination continues through adolescence and adulthood.

■ Differential Diagnosis

Developmental Coordination Disorder must be distinguished from other motor impairments that are due to a medical condition. Problems in coordination may be associated with specific neurological disorders (e.g., cerebral palsy, progressive lesions of the cerebellum), but in these cases, there is definite neural damage and abnormal findings on neurological examination. If Mental Retardation is present, Developmental Coordination Disorder can be diagnosed only if the motor difficulties are in excess of those usually associated with the mental retardation. A diagnosis of Developmental Coordination Disorder is not given if the criteria are met for a Pervasive Developmental Disorder. Individuals with Attention-Deficit/Hyperactivity Disorder may fall, bump into things, or knock things over, but this is usually due to distractibility and impulsiveness, rather than to a motor impairment. If criteria for both disorders are met, both diagnoses can be given. (*DSM-IV-TR*, pp. 56-58.)[2]

---

[2] Reprinted with permission from the *Diagnostic and Statistical Manual of Mental Disorders, Text Revision*, Copyright 2000. American Psychiatric Association.

Chapter Three

This description reveals that a full range and various types of motor problems may be evident in children with DCD. It also assumes that professionals measure the child's intelligence and use the IQ score or standard score for comparison with the child's motor abilities.

> *It is only possible to compare the findings of one's measured intelligence and motor abilities after both domains have been tested and the results have been converted into a standard score or index. Only then can one compare "apples to apples."*

What does that mean? It means that if someone notices significant motor skill difficulties in a child, and the motor problems seem to affect what the child can do at home or school, then further investigation should be conducted. If it is a teacher or therapist who notices these difficulties, this professional should talk to the child's parent – who, in turn, should talk to the family doctor or another specialist about this situation. That clinician or other professional should observe the child, gather extensive developmental history, and consider additional testing in the motor area or refer the child for appropriate assessment by another qualified professional, such as an OT or PT. If test results show, for example, that the child scores 115 on an IQ test but his motor quotient (as measured using another type of standardized test) is only 83, this shows a very significant difference between the two domains of behavior. In summary, these test results would show that the child's motor coordination is significantly less than or impaired when compared to his cognitive potential.

2 Criterion B

The disturbance in Criterion A significantly interferes with academic achievement or activities of daily living (ADL) (*DSM-IV-TR*, p. 58).

Academic achievement and *activities of daily living* will be explained separately to help you understand how motor difficulties impact different areas of life. Additional examples of motor skill problems that apply specifically to the classroom or home environment will be presented.

Chapter Three

Academic Achievement

Research has shown that school-aged children with DCD usually do much poorer in academic activities such as spelling, writing, and/or mathematics than their classmates who do not have DCD. These particular academic skills all require fine motor control with pens or pencils. A surprising research finding is that elementary-aged students spend 30-60 % of their school day in fine motor activities, most of which involve printing and writing. It follows naturally that if a child has difficulties with fine motor activities, she would quickly notice her weaker abilities and feel less capable than her classmates.

Generally, the written work of an individual with DCD is extremely messy and there is little to no consistency in the writing she produces. Work samples often reveal that the student has difficulty following and using margins and/or lines on the page and that she has trouble with appropriate spacing between letters and words. Production is often sparse. In addition, it is not uncommon to see very large and/or small letters as well as uppercase and lowercase letters used in the same word or sentence. Furthermore, tall letters, such as *b*, *d*, *h*, *l*, and *t*, may be the same height as short letters, such as *a*, *e*, *o*, and *u*. Vocabulary and word usage in written work is usually at a much more elementary level than what the student uses in her oral language skills. Spelling errors are also common in the writing samples of students with DCD.

I think the conferences are booGOOGring mor boring then frosen frensey. they are neseacrey. Not don't know what hapens in P.t.C. But I bo know it's hard to what for it to by orer.

Research also reveals other areas of difficulty when writing or printing. For example, the writing speed of students with DCD tends to be much slower than the writing speed of their peers without DCD. However, this is not always the case; some students race through their writing activities to get it over and done with quickly, and/or because they are too ashamed to let anyone else see the poor quality of their printing or writing. These same students may also be seen shielding or hiding their written work from others because they are embarrassed to let others see the quality of their printing or writing. In addition, because of difficulties with motor memory, students with DCD may form their letters inconsistently, or they may use a haphazard approach when printing or drawing.

Take a few minutes and closely watch your student print, write, and/or do math questions. Observe how the student forms letters and numbers and how frequently he pauses during these activities.

- Does he miss, substitute, or add extra letters to his words?

- Does he hold his head very near the paper while writing, as if he's watching to see what his hand and fingers are doing?

- Does he complain that his hand gets very tired after writing for a period of time?

- Does he use the traditional writing pattern of left-to-right and top-to-bottom, or does he use other unusual writing techniques, such as forming his letters from right-to-left or bottom-to-top?

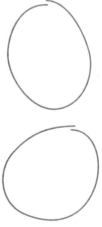

Students with fine motor coordination difficulties sometimes draw circles in a counterclockwise manner, and then moments later, they use a clockwise format. Lines may be created from the top down or from the bottom up. There does not seem to be any regularity to their penmanship.

In addition, it is not uncommon for a child with motor learning difficulties to hold her pencils and pens with very firm pressure (a "white-knuckle" grip). She may also use an inefficient pencil grip. The student might rest her head on the forearm of her non-writing hand while it is positioned on the desk, or she may prop her head in a supported position by cradling it in her non-writing hand.

This is especially true if the child has weak muscle tone. Propping her head in her hand for support allows the student to continue working longer. Otherwise, her body becomes too tired while she tries to maintain postural control. The child may also put her head down on the desktop or rest it on an outstretched forearm.

Overflow movements of the mouth may also accompany the handwriting activity. Overflow movements of the mouth involve nonfunctional oral-motor activities and/or tightening. For example, if overflow movements are expressed in the mouth region, one may observe the child opening and closing his lips without apparent purpose, holding the mouth in a tight but unusual formation, puckering his lips, thrusting his tongue, and/or performing any other movements of the tongue or lips. Overflow movements indicate that the child is using excessive cognitive energy to perform the task.

There are numerous sources that document the different types of pencil grips. They are usually identified in books on handwriting skills or resources written by OTs. Usually these descriptions are accompanied by pictures or simple diagrams of pencil grips. Most references suggest that there are three different types of grips that are considered efficient: tripod, adapted tripod, and quadrupod.

There is a simple way to analyze whether or not a grip is proficient. Does the individual manipulate his pencil using only his fingers, or does he hold the pencil in such a way that his finger and/or wrist position is locked in place? This is what is commonly observed in people who use an inefficient thumb-wrap, transpalmar, thumb tuck, interdigital brace, supinate, or index finger grip.

Inefficient grips such as these force the child to move his entire arm to create letter and number shapes. It is deemed inefficient because writing with locked finger or wrist action requires much more energy and larger muscle control than an optimal grip.

Note that overflow movements can also occur elsewhere (e.g., the non-writing hand positioned in a very tight fist or mirroring the writing actions, or the fingers may be held in a stiff and awkward manner).

Although most children with DCD are able to read and communicate effectively using oral language, they have extreme difficulty writing what they know onto paper. This difficulty is not because they have problems knowing what word to use or knowing what letter comes next in a word, for if you ask them, they are likely able to say the word they are trying to write, and they may even be able to spell the word orally. Rather, the problem is usually motor related. Many students with DCD need to pause slightly and think about how to form each letter as they are writing. Then, because cognitive energy is being used to recall how to form each specific letter, they forget what they were planning to write, producing simplistic and very brief work. It's just too tiring to do anything more than the basics!

Another problem that children with DCD may have is that they are unable to perceive what letter shape their hand is making when they write. They cannot form letters automatically (e.g., knowing how it feels to make the letter or number shapes). As a result, they may need to monitor what their hand is doing by watching it. The watching or examination of the hand action also requires additional time and cognitive effort. For instance, most of us could write a telephone number without looking at the paper. However, the person with DCD would have much more difficulty because she doesn't know what shape or design her hand is producing unless she looks at the product of her writing.

Some people test the child's ability to discern or sense shapes in the following manner.

• Use your pointer finger to write letter, number, or simple geometric shapes on the back of the child. Can the child discriminate what you have created?

• Ask the child to close his eyes. Guide his index or pointer finger to create other letter, number, or simple shapes on a paper or other textured surface. Can he tell you the shape that was created simply by feeling the action or knowing where and how his body moved in space? This activity will tell you whether or not his proprioceptive-kinesthetic feedback system is working optimally.

As part of the student's inconsistent motor actions, you may also notice that when these individuals cut paper with scissors, they approach the required cutting line from two different sides. Scissor action may be described as either very small, quick snips or a slow, large cutting action. Alternatively, the scissors may be held in such a manner that the student actually tears the paper rather than cutting it.

As mentioned earlier, students with DCD will probably experience difficulties with numerous motor activities at school. If, however, your child's motor difficulties only relate to printing and writing tasks and no other fine or gross motor skills, your child may have a learning disability in written expression rather than DCD.

Nevertheless, some students with DCD may be able to manage some school-related tasks with ease (e.g., reading, classroom discussions), and only display difficulties with the academic assignments involving handwriting and gross motor skills. Alternatively, they may do well in sports activities but exhibit major problems with almost all fine motor activities at school.

In the early elementary grades, fine motor activities typically involve folding, pasting, cutting, printing, drawing, coloring, and writing activities. In higher grades, other school-based fine motor tasks may include the following:

- handling laboratory equipment and performing experiments in science

- managing tools and conducting various tasks in industrial arts and other trade-related courses

- using utensils and performing other cooking skills, working with small appliances, doing hand-stitching, or working with sewing machines in home economics class

- combining sheets of papers with staples or into folders or placing daily worksheets in binders

Chapter Three

- constructing large posters, charts, and diagrams for various course requirements

- creating 3-D models to help understand geometry concepts in math

- using stencils, drawing, painting, sculpting, and creating other art projects

> *Although most children with DCD do not enjoy any type of arts or crafts, some children with DCD have less noticeable problems with drawing or other types of artwork. These students may actually enjoy art because there is no specific way to form lines, shapes, and express creativity with paper, pencil, brushes, and other art materials. In short, no one can tell a child that she is drawing a sunrise, tree, or mountain scene incorrectly. However, because of the specific ways that letters look and should be formed, it is possible to state that someone's writing is "neat and tidy" or else "messy and incorrect."*

Additional gross motor tasks related to school include the following:

- bending, reaching, stretching, placing and removing items from a desk, locker, etc.

- reorganizing desks, chairs, tables, etc., for group work projects in the classroom

- walking and finding one's way through the maze of school hallways and stairways

- setting up and removing large props in drama class

- carrying backpacks, books, and other educational supplies inside and out of the school

- appropriate participation as well as setting up and handling sports equipment in physical education class

In short, any combination of difficulties in gross and fine motor activities may be revealed at school.

Chapter Three

Activities of Daily Living

In addition to motor problems evidenced at school, self-care activities, leisure, and recreation pursuits at home or elsewhere can be negatively affected by poor coordination skills. These activities may include all types of toileting needs, meal preparation, eating, cleaning, dressing, etc. Many examples of such activities have already been presented in the checklists provided earlier in this book (pp. 55-56, 60-69). The following additional tasks are more geared to older adolescents at home or in a work environment:

- pouring hot and/or cold beverages into glasses and cups, preparing and serving snacks and meals

- picking up items, sweeping, vacuuming, dusting, and performing other house cleaning activities, such as folding laundry, hanging clothes on the line, and making beds

- mowing and/or raking leaves off the lawn, pruning hedges, and performing other landscaping tasks or outdoor yard work.

- writing a letter, including folding the paper, stuffing it in an envelope, and placing a stamp on the envelope

- turning doorknobs, dials, and faucets on and off; opening locked doors; chaining and locking bicycles and other objects

- walking the dog or caring for the family pet in other ways

- picking vegetables and fruit directly from plants or trees

- washing a car or truck, cleaning decks and siding, painting fences

- feeding, exercising, or caring for livestock

- buying, sorting, and placing foods in cabinets and the refrigerator

- setting the table, doing dishes by hand, or loading and emptying the dishwasher

Chapter Three

- shoveling snow off sidewalks and driveways

- chopping wood, lighting a campfire, setting up a tent, and/or performing other outdoor recreational activities

- driving a vehicle

3 Criterion C

The disturbance is not due to a medical condition (e.g., cerebral palsy, hemiplegia, or muscular dystrophy) and does not meet criteria for a pervasive developmental disorder (PDD) (*DSM-IV-TR*, p. 58).

Since some motor impairments are not actually DCD and may be due to certain medical conditions or some type of PDD, these conditions must be examined and rejected before diagnosing DCD. In addition, the diagnostic manual also reports that if a child is diagnosed with PDD, he should not be diagnosed with DCD.

For this very reason, it is important that the child's medical doctor is always consulted and that there are no apparent medical causes for the child's motor difficulties. In a psychologist's or other specialist's report, the clinician could add a statement such as: *"A telephone consultation with Dr. Lucian Burgess on September 23, 2005, confirmed that there are no known medical causes for (client's) motor difficulties."*

4 Criterion D

If mental retardation (MR) is present, the motor difficulties are in excess of those usually associated with retardation (*DSM-IV-TR*, p. 58).

This criterion suggests that it is possible for a child to have a dual diagnosis of MR and DCD. However, this seems contrary to the other *DSM-IV-TR* criteria, which state that the child must have average to above-average intelligence. Although the literature on DCD also recognizes that this combination of MR and DCD seems improbable and the joint diagnosis has been debated as being contradictory, if this applies to your child's situation, seek professional advice on this matter.

Chapter Three

▶ History of DCD

Children with motor difficulties likely existed before this condition was first documented in the literature. Nevertheless, they were not identified publicly in print until the early 1900s. At that time, children with motor coordination difficulties were described as having "congenital maladroitness." In the years that followed, they were referred to as "clumsy, awkward, slow, uncoordinated," and/or "having mild motor problems." In more recent years, these children may have been diagnosed as having "developmental dyspraxia, minimal brain dysfunction, a psychomotor syndrome, minimal cerebral palsy, sensory integrative problems," and/or "clumsy child syndrome." Even terms such as *perceptual-motor impairment*, *apraxia*, and *nonverbal learning disorder* have been used to describe this population.

In 1987, the American Psychiatric Association (APA) recognized a distinct disorder involving movement skills and abilities. Two years later, the World Health Organization (WHO) endorsed a similar condition. Since then – and until the present time – two distinctly different diagnostic terms have been used which seemingly describe the same condition. The WHO, in their 1992 diagnostic manual *The International Classification of Diseases 10 (ICD-10)*, used the term *specific developmental disorder of motor function*, while the *Diagnostic and Statistical Manual - Text Revision (DSM-TR)* published in 1994 by the APA referred to a comparable condition as *developmental coordination disorder*. Although the criteria in the original *ICD-10* and *DSM-IV* differed, much of the requirements for diagnosis are similar. Nevertheless, it is impressive to think that both of these influential agencies recognize that motor coordination problems are worthy of identification and intervention!

The difference in terminology created a great deal of confusion among people and researchers working in this field. As a result, in 1994 at the International Consensus Meeting on Children and Clumsiness held at London, Ontario, Canada, the term *developmental coordination disorder (DCD)* was adopted as the official name for this disability among researchers and clinicians. Finally, DCD was internationally recognized as a distinct entity. It is interesting to note that the diagnostic criteria have remained exactly the same from 1994 until now.

Chapter Three

Fortunately, even before *DCD* was officially recognized as the term to use in official literature, a tremendous amount of research had been conducted on children with this condition. Since the 1970s, scientists and other professionals have been studying this topic extensively, and investigations continue to the present time. For example, scientists and researchers working in many different disciplines from all over the world (e.g., Australia, Finland, Italy, The Netherlands, Brazil, France, England, Sweden, Belgium, Ireland, Switzerland, Singapore, Nigeria, New Zealand, United States of America, Wales, Germany, Norway, South Africa, Japan) have discovered many interesting findings.

Researchers to date have determined the following information:

- It is possible to measure significant delays in motor skills.

- Motor coordination difficulties are present in approximately five to eight percent of the general population.

- Children with DCD are a heterogeneous group; there is great variation among children with DCD and in what is causing the difficulty. Individuals vary in sex, age, race, gender, socio-economic ability, etc., and they do not all have the same types of motor coordination problems.

- DCD is more common in boys than girls. Some studies suggest that the proportion is as high as four boys to one girl.

- DCD may be caused by any single difficulty or combination of difficulties in visual processing (especially visual-spatial tasks), motor memory, motor planning, proprioceptive-kinesthetic feedback, balance, etc.

- Children with DCD seem at a disadvantage when required to respond quickly.

- DCD is a life-long condition that is best addressed with early intervention.

- One of the primary indicators is very messy handwriting.

- Metacognitive interventions are proving to be effective.

- Numerous children with DCD also have difficulty with haptic (touch) skills. Without looking or using a visual reference, many of these children have difficulty grasping, holding, and/or feeling an object only with their hands and knowing what it is. For instance, if a child places his hand inside a covered box or under a tabletop, he may have trouble distinguishing shapes, textures, and sizes of items, such as distinguishing a wooden block from a cardboard, pyramid-shaped object.

- Children as young as age six can already tell that their motor skills are inferior when compared to their peers, and this knowledge starts to affect their self-esteem.

- If your child has DCD, she may or may not also have other conditions. This overlap of conditions is referred to as *co-existing disorders* or *comorbidity*. There tends to be a high frequency of children who also experience learning disabilities and/or attention problems along with the DCD diagnosis. Therefore, the presence or absence of other conditions, and even the diagnosis of DCD, must be investigated carefully by qualified professionals.

- Although some people try to reassure worried parents that their child with motor coordination problems will "grow out of it" without intervention, motor skill difficulties do not go away on their own, nor will the person eventually catch up. During adolescence, however, boys with motor skill problems seem less affected than when they were younger.

- Over time, people with motor coordination difficulties start to isolate themselves from their peers and to withdraw socially. Anxiety is a common problem in early adolescence. Although it does not affect all students in the same way, research shows that it is quite common for people with motor skill problems to develop physical and mental health issues.

- On standardized intelligence tests, children with DCD often score significantly higher in verbal skills than on performance or perceptual reasoning tasks, especially when the items are timed. Some researchers even suggested that the Verbal Scale score alone (on the older *WICS-III*) should be used as an indicator of cognitive ability, for by including the Performance Scale score in the Full Scale score, a child's IQ may appear much lower than it likely is. In essence, when the nonverbal score is low, the student is penalized for difficulties with fine motor

Chapter Three

and visual-spatial skills. Since some children also have expressive language difficulties, however, the verbal score on the IQ tests can also be a very poor measure of a child's actual ability. Fortunately, the *WISC-IV* does not use speed as much in its measurement of perceptual reasoning as it used to. Regardless, because some children are affected by speech and/or visual-spatial difficulties and motor problems, they may score much lower on verbal tasks, perceptual reasoning tasks, and processing speed (which involves the use of fine motor control with paper and pencil). Hence, decisions based exclusively on IQ scores must be treated with caution.

- There are some remarkable similarities between DCD, nonverbal learning disability (NVLD), and Asperger syndrome (AS). Students described as having developmental dyspraxia, sensory integrative dysfunction (SID), or as the "out-of-sync child," are all reported to have some combination of difficulties with motor coordination, social skill difficulties, and visual spatial deficits. There seems to be much overlap in some of these terms, and various professionals appear to use different terms to describe the same population. Nevertheless, NVLD, AS, SID, developmental dyspraxia, and other such named conditions are considered to be deficiencies primarily in social and other interpersonal skills with some motor difficulties. In contrast, DCD is considered to be more of a motor deficiency that, over time, impacts social skills. These terms and conditions will be discussed in greater detail later in this chapter (pp. 108-122).

▶ Making a Diagnosis of DCD

Based on the criteria in the *DSM-IV-TR*, only medical doctors, pediatricians, psychiatrists, and chartered psychologists are able to make the diagnosis of DCD. It is important that these professionals have some training and background in the motor domain. If they do not have knowledge about motor skills, they will depend on the reports and insights from others who have tested the client's proficiency in various motor skills.

Before making any diagnosis, professionals should always gather numerous pieces of evidence.

Chapter Three

As always, before making any diagnosis, professionals should always gather numerous pieces of evidence. For a very thorough assessment, the qualified clinician must first inquire about the child's developmental history, then ask about or explore the presence or absence of neurological or other medical difficulties. Next, the clinician should assess, refer for assessment, or review current results of the child's intellectual ability. In addition, the clinician needs to gather data on the child's performance of gross and fine motor skills at school and at home, and the quality of the child's motor ability.

An assessment of the child's motor ability may be done in several ways, including a thorough observation of the child in multiple settings where motor performance is expected, by specific motor assessments using standard-ized tests and instruments, and/or by criteria-referenced assessments.

Parents may also be asked to complete various rating scales and checklists. It is also extremely helpful if the parent or caregiver prepares a list of activities that the child has trouble doing. Emphasis should be on tasks that impact the child's functioning at school or self-help skills at home.

Standardized tests must be administered in the exact same manner each time they are conducted (e.g., the standards of administration, such as the material, scoring, and other procedures, are always the same). That way the data can be compared to other children with similar features (e.g., age, grade level, social-economic status, gender).

In contrast, criterion-referenced assess-ments are designed to measure how well the child performs a specific task or criteria (e.g., when performing a two-foot jump, does the child bend the knees, lean forward, use arm thrust?). The child is judged against the optimum level of skill performance – not by the skill of anyone else.

If the professional is unable to examine the child's motor domain directly, assessment findings from an OT and/or PT could also be used. This information must be analyzed carefully and much clinical judgment is required. Hopefully, you will find a clinician who knows about DCD and has the training, skills, and access to the assessment tools needed to make a diagnosis.

One way or another, the assessment process must be thorough! You should be concerned if you meet with a doctor, psychiatrist, or psychologist and walk out with a diagnosis of DCD (or any other condition, for that matter) after a 10-to-15-minute office visit.

• **DCD Diagnosis Beyond 18 Years**

The *DSM-IV-TR* classifies DCD under the heading "Disorders Usually First Diagnosed in Infancy, Childhood, or Adolescence." Although the diagnosis of DCD is usually made before the age of 18, generally the diagnosis stays with the person for life, as it does for a youngster diagnosed with MR, AD/HD, or Asperger syndrome (AS). The condition itself does not change significantly as one gets older; rather, the person usually finds better ways to cope with her difficulties and ends up choosing a career that suits her skills and interests. Still, one does not stop having features of these conditions upon becoming an adult.

In the same way, individuals who have DCD do not typically stop having motor coordination problems when they turn 18 years of age. Research has shown that without a successful intervention program, a person who has a tendency to be clumsy and uncoordinated in childhood most often continues to struggle with the same types of motor coordination difficulties as an adult. An interesting twist occurs, though. If motor coordination difficulties do not appear to affect the performance of one's self-care activities and academic or work-related tasks, then by definition, the person does not have DCD anymore. The impact of motor problems on activities of daily living, if you recall, is the critical piece needed for the DCD diagnosis.

For example, if a 25-year-old has learned to perform all necessary self-care activities (e.g., is able to manage basic meal preparation, personal hygiene, perform all schoolwork or employment assignments on a computer, and simply does not get involved in sporting or other athletic pursuits for recreation), then by strict definition, he does not have DCD. He may, in fact, still have coordination difficulties, despite the fact that he has learned to adapt very well. As he gets older, he may end up in a successful career in which motor proficiency is not needed; then there may be no other observable evidence of motor difficulties. Essentially, the person would still have an underlying coordination problem without anyone knowing. The question then is, would it matter if the individual had the diagnosis if it did not seem to impact life at home and work? You decide.

Numerous case studies and research findings show how troublesome it can be for adults who have struggled with undiagnosed motor coordination difficulties for years. Although these individuals may have been prescribed medication and treated for psychiatric problems, and may have struggled with many other aspects of life (e.g., self-worth, confidence, academic achievement, motivation for career goals, and interpersonal skills), some of them come to realize that their underlying difficulties have never been addressed properly. Fortunately there are some reports from Great Britain indicating that, even at an older age, some of these people have participated in intervention programs that have offered success.

■ Other Conditions That Affect Motor Coordination

As mentioned earlier, DCD is not the only disorder that affects motor skill performance. The following will be a brief overview of some of the other conditions that also affect motor coordination.

▶ Attention Deficit/Hyperactivity Disorder (AD/HD)

AD/HD is another condition identified in the *DSM-IV-TR*. There are actually three main types of AD/HD. Because of the letter *H* in AD/HD, many people think that if their child is not "hyper" or overly active, the child does not have attention problems. However, that is not true. Some people use the term *ADD* to refer to the "inattentive" or "daydreaming" student. Even though it is used frequently in society, the abbreviation *ADD* does not follow the *DSM-IV-TR* guidelines exactly. It has simply become a convenient way to indicate the non-hyper type of AD/HD. A more correct way to identify the different types of attention problems is as follows:

- AD/HD (Primarily the hyperactive/impulsive type)

- AD/HD (Primarily the inattentive type) – This is what people typically mean when they refer to ADD.

- AD/HD (Combined type) – For this diagnosis, there must be six or more features of hyperactive and impulsive behaviors, as well as six or more features of inattentive behaviors evident in the last six months.

Chapter Three

The *DSM-IV-TR* includes the diagnostic criteria for these three conditions, but for the purposes of this book, following is a short explanation of similarities and differences between the motor proficiencies of an individual with DCD vs. AD/HD.

Sometimes a child with challenges in the motor domain may appear to have DCD, yet the child actually has a problem with attention. For example, a child may trip over objects, appear clumsy, spill things, or make other motor mistakes because she is simply daydreaming, not paying attention to details, or in a hurry to get somewhere. The child's impulsivity, lack of self-control, or passive approach to tasks creates the motor problems. One way to tell the difference between DCD and AD/HD is that the child who has problems with attention will probably be able to perform various motor tasks properly some of the time, as the child's tendency to be easily distracted and her lack of focus or concentration on what she is doing may result in the seemingly clumsy and uncoordinated movements. In contrast, the child with DCD will seldom be to able to perform motor tasks properly and/or consistently, whether or not she is distracted or focusing on and attending to the motor task.

Additionally, students with attention problems often have a difficult time recalling instructions or multi-step directions. They may appear unable to perform a motor skill properly, but have actually forgotten the sequence with which they were to perform the skills. Although the child with DCD may also have similar problems paying attention (recall that many students with DCD also have co-morbid conditions, one which is AD/HD), he may actually remember the sequence but perform the motor skill in the wrong order because of motor planning difficulties.

There are many other references which offer greater insight into the details of AD/HD. If this interests you, you are encouraged to seek out and read those articles/books on your own. Here are two resources to consider:

- Richard, G.J. & Russell, J.L. (2001). *The Source for ADD/ADHD*. East Moline, IL: LinguiSystems, Inc.

- Richard, G.J. (2001). *The Source for Processing Disorders*. East Moline, IL: LinguiSystems, Inc.

Chapter Three

▶ Learning Disorders

The *DSM-IV-TR* reports, "Learning Disorders may also be associated with a higher rate of Developmental Coordination Disorder" (p. 50). There are several types of learning disorders/disabilities. The type that seems most closely aligned with DCD involves written expression and math. As a matter of fact, there is some research showing that many children with DCD are good readers and can comprehend and explain what they have learned. They simply have trouble documenting that knowledge on paper in ways that most teachers expect them to.

Printing or writing is an extremely complex activity. It requires a great deal of physical control and multiple cognitive processes. For example, before being truly ready to write, students must have done all of the following:

- developed postural control

- acquired good hand-eye coordination

- established hand dominance

- learned how to move, coordinate, and control the small muscles of the hand

- developed the ability to execute a motor plan

- established perceptual organization and visual discrimination (e.g., knowledge of how to use and recognize differences in letters, numbers, and other symbols)

- acquired adequate language processing skills (e.g., the ability to understand the associations between letters and sounds)

- generated a mental image of a word or symbol before putting pencil to paper

- understood what they intend to communicate

- developed the ability to control where and how letters are formed and written on lined paper, know when to make spaces between words, and how to mark the ends of sentences

Chapter Three

One need only add problems with coordination to this mix, and you can see how challenging writing is for the student with motor difficulties!

Although most students with DCD are usually diagnosed with learning disorders (LD) in written expression, this is not always the case. Two completely different scenarios follow.

1 If a student has a great deal of trouble with all kinds of motor skills and cannot write sentences or paragraphs that are clearly understood, and the student's work is excessively messy, that individual is likely to be diagnosed with DCD and LD in written expression.

2 Now consider another student who is able to construct good sentences and organized paragraphs with proper grammar, spelling, variation in sentence structure, and appropriate punctuation, but the work is very messy, spacing problems are evident, and the rate of production is painstakingly slow. This student may be diagnosed with DCD but not LD. It appears that his ability to express himself with writing is fine; it's just that his motor problems are creating difficulties with production. Nevertheless, because most students with DCD have such significant problems with writing, it only seems right to provide them with the accommodations they need for state, provincial, or national examinations. The second student with such motor difficulties may still need to be identified as having a learning disability in written expression to access a scribe and more time for state or provincial government examinations.

> The student with significant motor difficulties may still need to be identified as having a learning disability in written expression to access a scribe and more time for state, provincial, or national examinations.

Furthermore, not all students with LD in writing have DCD. Take Vigard, for example. He and his family immigrated to the United States from Finland about six years ago. Vigard is a very capable boy who easily learned the English language. His social skills are good and he has no difficulty understanding the academic content of his current fifth-grade placement. However, he has trouble reading. Furthermore, Vigard is able to manage most fine motor and gross motor skills with ease and, if asked to reproduce some numbers, letters, or symbols, he tries his best and the resultant work is actually quite neat. However, because of problems with perceptual organization, visual discrimination, and language processing skills, he is unable to read and/or document what he knows. His writing difficulties are due to problems with the decoding and encoding of symbols and letters, which one requires to read and write the English language. In this case, his writing difficulties have nothing to do with problems in the motor domain. As a result, he should be diagnosed with LD in written expression, but not DCD.

Some children with DCD and/or writing difficulties also have problems with arithmetic. Although most math problems are documented in a left-to-right, horizontal fashion, others are written in a top-down vertical format. For students who have trouble maintaining columns and rows when performing math calculations, this can result in confusion and incorrect answers to questions. Once again, problems with motor control, visual processing, and spatial orientation are confusing the child's ability to document what she knows.

▶ Nonverbal Learning Disability (NLD or NVLD)

Although many people use *NLD* to indicate nonverbal learning disability, these three letters are also used at times to refer to another group of people. *NLD* indicates "non-learning disabled" in the scientific literature when comparisons are made between samples of students who are learning disabled (LD) and non-learning disabled. Therefore, to reduce any confusion, *NVLD* will be used in this resource.

Chapter Three

- **Definition and Diagnosis**

  NVLD is a term used to describe students who struggle with nonverbal tasks. This means that, in contrast to students with learning disabilities who typically struggle with reading, writing, math, and sometimes oral language skills (e.g., "verbal" tasks), children with NVLD are usually reported as having age-appropriate to very good verbal skills. Although people promoting this disorder report that children with NVLD share a common set of features (e.g., motor coordination problems, social skill delays, and visual-spatial processing difficulties), **NVLD does not currently have a specific criteria for diagnosis**. Furthermore, when attending conferences or workshops on the topic of NVLD, it is very difficult to get any presenter to state exactly how a diagnosis is made. This lack of uniform criteria results in much confusion and controversy among professionals and parents.

- **History of NVLD**

  NVLD is a relatively new term that was developed by Dr. Byron Rourke in the 1980s. Since then, Dr. Rourke has worked tirelessly with many of his graduate students to develop this topic of interest. Research findings are generated primarily in Canada, but many parents, teachers, and other professionals throughout North America are now promoting this diagnosis. The late Sue Thompson, a speech-language pathologist, via her LinguiSystems book on this topic[3], helped to popularize NVLD. Now many conferences, workshops, and schools are developing programs to deal with this population.

A review of the material being promoted for children with NVLD typically focuses on the development of skills in the social domain because that seems to be the greatest area of deficit. However, many of the motor learning strategies presented in this book will likely work very successfully with children with NVLD because these students have the ability to reason and understand information, especially when it is presented using verbal mediation. Furthermore, because the literature on NVLD recognizes that these students struggle with motor learning and performance and it is very difficult to find information about how to intervene in this domain, this resource is a critical part of intervention for the student diagnosed with NVLD.

---

[3] Thompson, S. (1997). *The Source for Nonverbal Learning Disorders*. East Moline, IL: LinguiSystems, Inc.

Chapter Three

At the present time, it appears that NVLD is being used in two distinct manners, the implications of which are quite different. First, some people employ *NVLD* as an umbrella term to describe any student who struggles with nonverbal skills, such as social skills, motor proficiency, and/or visual-spatial abilities. For instance, when a clinician cannot distinguish exactly what is causing a child's difficulties in these areas, and the professional is uncertain of how to present the information to the child's parents, she may choose to use the term *NVLD* to identify the grouping of deficits.

Under this nebulous NVLD umbrella, there is a full range of difficult behaviors. For example, some students may display significant sensory problems, social deficits, and/or features more consistent with a diagnosis of Asperger syndrome (AS). On the other side of the umbrella, there may be students who struggle primarily with motor difficulties and visual-spatial deficits.

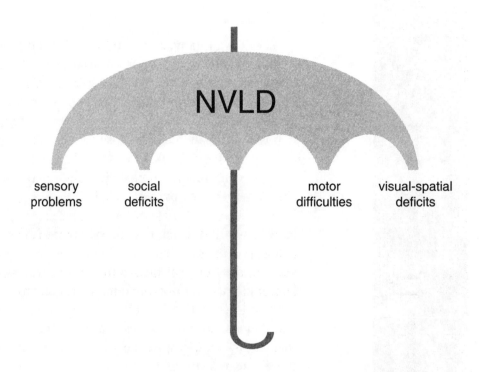

Second, NVLD has taken on a life of its own. There are professionals who are using *NVLD* to mean that the child has a specific and identifiable condition distinct from any other, even when the diagnostic criteria are not clear and/or used consistently.

At times the decision to diagnose NVLD is rather simplistic. For instance, I have read many reports and have heard numerous professionals talk about a child being diagnosed NVLD because his measured verbal comprehension score on a cognitive assessment is significantly stronger than his performance (or perceptual reasoning) score. Although the literature warns about such inappropriate practices, the reality is that it occurs much more than individuals would like to acknowledge.

As a matter of fact, the stronger verbal over performance score was part of Rourke's initial diagnostic criteria in the 1980s. Now, however, that has changed. For example, in documentation received at a 2005 conference on NVLD, it was reported that only 27% of students "provisionally classified" as having NVLD have higher Verbal scores than Performance scores on the *WISC*. The difference between Verbal and Performance scores only had to be ten points, a variation that is not even one standard deviation, based on statistics provided by the test developer (Wechsler). Students trained to conduct Wechsler intelligence tests such as the *WISC-III* and the current *WISC-IV*, were taught that the standard deviation on this test was 15 points, meaning that you need a 15-point or more spread in order for a "significant discrepancy" to be present. Hence, it is possible that there are some students whose Verbal and Performance scores actually fall inside the same range, yet some people refer to these students as having NVLD.

Furthermore, people have used just a checklist to promote or seek an NVLD diagnosis for their children or students in their classes. In addition, some reports reveal that clinicians have made the NVLD diagnosis if the child has minor motor and social difficulties, even if visual processing is not affected. To date, no one has been able to describe the degree of impairment and which one, two, or three domains must be affected to make a diagnosis legitimate. As a result, there is much confusion and inconsistency in the field. In fact, in the next section you will read that NVLD appears to have many similarities with other *DSM-IV-TR* conditions.

▶ Asperger Syndrome (AS)

Asperger syndrome (AS) is a specific condition that is part of the pervasive developmental disorders (PDD). Another more common term for the PDD condition is *autistic spectrum disorders*. AS has become fairly well known in professional circles over the last five years, and it is not uncommon to hear that an acquaintance's child, a specific student in school, or other individual has been diagnosed with AS. For the purposes of this book, a brief overview of Asperger syndrome and how it compares to NVLD will be presented. Of course, the types of motor problems these children experience will also be discussed.

The term *Asperger syndrome* was named after an Austrian psychiatrist named Hans Asperger. In 1944, he wrote a paper in which he described similar features in 200 people that he had seen in his medical practice. Since the original paper was written in German, the contents were not well known or understood until it was translated many years later. In 1981, Lorna Wing summarized several other translations of Asperger's work and added to that original document by commenting on her work with 34 other individuals ranging in ages from five to 35 years of age. According to Wing, these children and adults displayed differences in speech, nonverbal communication, and social interactions, as well as a preference for repetitive activities and a resistance to change, unique skills and interests, and different experiences in school. Over the years, many other authors have learned and written about AS, and now there is no shortage of resources on this topic.

▶ NVLD and Asperger Syndrome (AS)

Scholars and clinicians have discovered remarkable similarities among DCD and NVLD and AS. For example, students diagnosed with DCD or NVLD and/or AS are all reported to have some problems with motor coordination, social skill difficulties, and visual spatial processing. The subtle differences (and possible similarities) among these conditions follow.

DCD is considered to be primarily a motor learning disorder that starts to affect psychosocial development and interpersonal skills by the early elementary years. The clumsy child (who may or may not be diagnosed as having DCD) recognizes she is motorically much less capable than her peers. To save the embarrassment when classmates do not invite her to play at recess, this student often chooses to withdraw so her weak motor skills will not be evident to others. However, her social interaction skills are good; she can create and read nonverbal cues and gestures the same as her peers. She already understands that she won't be included in play scenarios, so she chooses to prevent an awkward social situation by purposefully isolating herself from her classmates.

In contrast, NVLD and AS are often referred to as *social skill disorders*. Rourke, the pioneer researcher in NVLD, reports that social skill difficulties start to become apparent at about eight years of age, although before the student is eight years old, the child is already identified as having some peculiarities. Throughout Sue Thompson's 1997 book on NVLD, many of the case studies and descriptions of NVLD sound strangely like features of children with AS. Without specific training in diagnosing social skills disorders, motor conditions, and visual-spatial abilities, it is very difficult for untrained clinicians to identify exact differences between these conditions with certainty. It could be that the term *NVLD* had been heard and used in professional circles just prior to people hearing about AS. Alternatively, it may be that NVLD has become a "politically correct" way to inform parents that their child has a problem without being forthright about the true diagnosis. It is much easier to explain to parents that their child has a nonverbal learning disability than to tell them that their child has features consistent with a type of Autism Spectrum Disorder. NVLD may be considered a less severe form of AS.

One way or another, to date, this writer has not yet found any professional who (or other resource which) can clearly differentiate the difference between AS and NVLD. Although there have been and continue to be attempts to differentiate NVLD and AS, at a conference in Canada in 2005, Katherine Tsatsanis, who was a student of Byron Rourke and now works as a researcher at the Yale Child Study Center, stated, "Many but not all individuals with AS have NVLD." Then she added, "Most children with NVLD do not have AS." Although most of her initial presentation was on the differences between high functioning Autism and AS, she also presented some data on the "Provisional rules of classification for NVLD" – a summary of work conducted by Pelletier, Ahmad, and Rourke (2001) [cited by Tsatsanis]. Unfortunately, the list developed by Pelletier, Ahmad, and Rourke is based on older assessment tools. Psychologists and other clinicians are always encouraged to begin working with new assessment tools as soon as norms are available for the population they work with. Hence, much of Pelletier and co-worker's findings are already outdated.

Because of the diagnostic uncertainty between AS and NVLD, I do not use NVLD as a diagnosis in my clinical work; however, I do and will continue to use AS as a diagnostic term. Nevertheless, there are distinct differences between DCD and AS and/or NVLD, as outlined on page 118.

Chapter Three

AS / NVLD	DCD
considered socially odd	aware of/pained by social isolation
may or may not want friends	clearly wants friends
fascinated by unique topics of interest	interested in "regular kid stuff"
may have splinter skills (can perform some skills with great proficiency and others not at all)	may or may not have problems in multiple motor skills – however, the child is generally "klutzy"
does not understand social cues	understands social gestures/actions
play habits consist of solitary, parallel, or repetitive actions, setting up "worlds" and environments, scripted scenarios	progresses through normal stages of play: imaginative, social, cooperative, and competitive
may rock, or display specific nonfunctional motor mannerisms	does not typically display nonfunctional motor activity, just awkward ones
difficulty distinguishing fact from fiction; doesn't comprehend "it's a story"	knows the differences between truth and created information
verbal style is very talkative, clearly articulated, and detailed in content	verbal style may be minimal, sloppy, or lethargic; takes "too much effort"
may be hyper- or hypo-sensitive to light, sound, texture, smell, taste, etc.	doesn't often display extreme sensitivity to environmental conditions
often has linguistic differences (voice sounds peculiar and pedantic, problems with semantics and natural conversation)	language differences may be due to poor pronunciation and articulation (problems with oral motor control)
may not understand literal comments	can comprehend meanings/humor of jokes
socially and emotionally awkward	uses emotions properly

Of course the student does not need to have all of the conditions listed in order to be identified as having NVLD, AS, or DCD. However, most of these features would likely apply in order for a diagnosis to be made.

In summary, if one is not using NVLD as an umbrella term but rather as a distinct entity, it might be that NVLD and AS are indeed one and the same condition – just differing in severity. AS and NVLD may simply be called different disorders by people in different professions. In contrast, I hope you have come to understand that DCD is slightly different. One way or another, it seems that, based on the specific diagnosis (NVLD and/or AS, compared to DCD), there should be a totally different approach.

Finally, one last comment about the possible cause of confusion among many people regarding DCD, AS, and NVLD. The problems people have when differentiating varying types of disorders may be in part the result of differences between graduate training programs in Europe and North America. A short explanation follows.

Although psychologists in Europe and other countries of the world learn about the importance of the psychomotor domain, this topic is seldom dealt with in graduate schools for psychologists in North America. Rather, the focus in psychology within this continent is to learn about and examine the cognitive and affective domains, even though a taxonomy of educational objectives was developed by Bloom, Krathwohl, and Masia approximately 40 years ago (Gallahue and Ozmun; 1995). Bloom and co-workers were very clear about the interconnectedness between the affective, cognitive, and psychomotor domains.

> In this book, the term psychomotor follows Kerr's definition as summarized by Kamps (2000). "Psychomotor learning is a psychological approach which focuses on how motor skills are learned and performed. By observing human motor behaviors, one seeks to construct models which explain how that behavior is produced." (p. 10)

However, without proper training and expertise in the psychomotor domain, it is very difficult for professionals to assess and then address what the real underlying issue may be in children with social, motor, and visual processing problems. Due to a lack of training in and about the motor domain, it is very probable that motor coordination problems are actually more significant than reported by current clinicians. Because professionals do not typically assess the motor domain, there tends to be a greater focus on social skill deficits and, therefore, more identification of NVLD and/or AS than DCD.

Chapter Three

Note that NVLD is primarily a North American phenomenon. It may be that because of Rourke's work in Canada from the 1980s to the present time, NVLD has become popularized in Canadian provinces and American states. In contrast, AS is known and recognized more globally. This is also very true for DCD, as there is a large international body of knowledge on this topic.

It is possible that DCD, AS, and NVLD are all distinct entities, as some claim. Certainly this topic deserves more research. If one can put aside the controversy of differentiating among the various conditions, the underlying fact remains the same: students with deficits in various areas deserve and need assistance in those weak areas. One way or another, the strategies in this book will assist students who have been diagnosed as having NVLD, AS, or DCD.

> *If one can put aside the controversy of differentiating among the various conditions, the underlying fact remains the same: students with deficits in various areas deserve and need assistance in those weak areas.*

The confusion among AS, NVLD, and DCD does not stop here. Other terms such as the *out-of-sync child, sensory integrative dysfunction (SID)*, and other similar identifiers are used routinely by certain professions and individuals. When other professionals hear these terms, they may be very skeptical because they are unclear about the diagnostic criteria and the ways one condition is different from another. Once again, it is very possible that different professionals are using different terms to identify the same condition in a child.

For example, it may be that because some professions are not permitted to diagnose conditions within the *DSM-IV-TR*, new terms have been created to help parents understand that their child does indeed display a specific area of difficulty. However, the terms these different professionals use may vary. For example, a child psychiatrist may identify a young boy as having AS, an SLP or psychologist may use the term *NVLD* to describe the child's difficulties, and an occupational therapist may identify the same youngster as having SID or say he is an out-of-sync child. The use of the above terms by different professionals may be compounded by the fact that one specific clinician is trained in her particular discipline and thus focuses on one main domain of development, rather than having detailed knowledge of many different domains and conditions. One way or another, many children identified as having SID often exhibit other features that appear somewhat related to AS. And, as one reads or hears information about the out-of-sync child, many of these descriptions also seem related to AS.

So, even though most people recognize that there are distinct (or subtle) differences among each child they see, and one youngster may display more or less of a certain feature, the literature is still very unclear about which factors must be present (and to what degree) in order to substantiate a diagnosis of AS, NVLD, SID, or the out-of-sync child. It is possible that clinicians want to identify problem areas without a specific *DSM-IV-TR* diagnosis and, therefore, terms such as *NVLD*, *SID*, and *out-of-sync child* are developed. These terms may be closely related to each other, yet very different from DCD.

▶ The Slow Learner

Although not true for every single child, the literature is quite clear that a student identified as intellectually deficient or as a "slow learner" often displays problems in motor skills. In addition, that same individual usually has delays in social skills, speech, adaptive skills, and other independent functioning. This student typically requires a much different teaching approach when learning motor skills. Tasks must be presented very simply, and only a few functional skills should be taught at a time. Often hand-over-hand or another similar physical action is used to show the child how movements feel. For example, a teacher may demonstrate, then perform a trial movement with a student, and then repeat the motion numerous times until the child starts to acquire and practice the movement using proper motor form. Lots of practice and repetition is generally helpful.

Although some of the strategies in the next chapter may work with the child who has been diagnosed as a slow learner, there are also other books and resources available that suggest teaching strategies for these children. While the primary focus of this book is to help children who have average to above-average intellectual abilities, several of these strategies have also worked well to teach fundamental motor skills to preschoolers with Down syndrome. In fact, because research shows that children with Down syndrome are more delayed in motor skills than cognitive skills, using these children's relative strength in cognitive processing to teach motor skills has yielded very positive results.

Chapter Three

■ Summary

This chapter presented four main topics. First, two case studies showed that even trained clinicians may miss the true cause of children's difficulties. Fortunately, with more information about DCD and how it affects various domains of behavior, parents and other professionals will be better able to identify these problems sooner and, hopefully, provide children with the intervention that suits their difficulties.

It is necessary to measure a child's cognitive skills as part of gathering pertinent information for an overall assessment. The second section of this chapter reviewed intelligence testing in detail to clarify the terms and meaning of a cognitive assessment. This basic background knowledge helps one to proceed with the assessment process and determine which diagnosis best describes the child's difficulties. In order to qualify for a DCD diagnosis, the child must have average to above-average measured intelligence.

The third section presented the official description of DCD, its diagnostic features, the history of DCD, and information about making a diagnosis of DCD. The *DSM-IV-TR* criteria are reviewed, basic research findings are highlighted, and historical information about DCD is identified.

The last section described other conditions that affect motor skill acquisition and ability, including attention deficit/hyperactivity disorder (AD/HD), learning disabilities (LD), nonverbal learning disabilities (NVLD) and/or Asperger syndrome (AS), the out-of-sync child, sensory integrative dysfunction (SID), and the slow learner. Professionals must have a solid understanding of various diagnostic criteria and know how one condition is similar to or different from another.

Even for the child who has been diagnosed as intellectually deficient, the strategies that follow in Chapter Four will be beneficial to each diagnostic group identified above. Using their relative area of strength (cognitive reasoning ability), the individual with AD/HD, NVLD, AS, the out-of-sync child, and/or the youngster with SID should all be able to learn and profit from the various strategies presented in the next chapter.

Chapter Three

References

- Adreon, D., & Stella, J. (2001). Transition to middle and high school: Increasing the success of students with Asperger syndrome. *Intervention in School and Clinic, 36*(5), 266-271.

- American Psychiatric Association (1987). *Diagnostic and statistical manual of mental disorders (3rd ed. revised).* Washington, DC: Author.

- American Psychiatric Association (1994). *Diagnostic and statistical manual of mental disorders (4th ed.).* Washington, DC: Author.

- American Psychiatric Association (2000). *Diagnostic and statistical manual of mental disorders (4th ed. – text revision).* Washington, DC: Author.

- Attwood, T. (1998). *Asperger's syndrome: A guide for parents and professionals.* London: Jessica Kingsley Publishers.

- Attwood, T. (2000, Nov. 15). Effective strategies to aid social/emotional development for more able individuals with Autism and Asperger's syndrome. Calgary, AB, Canada: Presentation sponsored by Geneva Centre for Autism.

- Ayres, A.J. (1979). *Sensory integration and the child.* Los Angeles, CA: Western Psychological Services.

- Barnett, A.L., Kooistra, L., & Henderson, S.E. (Eds.) (1998). Clumsiness as syndrome and symptom. In H.T.A. Whiting & M.G. Whiting (Eds.), *Human Movement Science, 17*(4-5).

- Barnhill, G.P. (2001). What is Asperger's syndrome? *Intervention in School and Clinic, 36*(5), 259-265.

- Beek, P.J., & van Wieringen, P.C.W. (Eds.) (2001). *Human Movement Science, 20*(1-2).

- Bock, M.A. (2001). SODA strategy: Enhancing the social interaction skills of youngsters with Asperger syndrome. *Intervention in School and Clinic, 36*(5), 272-278.

- Brownell, M.T., & Walther-Thomas, C. (2001). Steven Shore: Understanding the autism spectrum: What teachers need to know. *Intervention in School and Clinic, 36*(5), 293-299, 305.

Chapter Three

- Cermak, S.A., & Larkin, D. (Eds.) (2002). *Developmental coordination disorder*. Clifton Park, NY: Thompson Delmar Learning.

- Fox, A.M., & Lent, B. (1996). Clumsy children: Primer on developmental coordination disorder. *Canadian Family Physician, 42*, 1965-1971.

- Gallahue, D.L., & Ozman, J.C. (2005). *Understanding motor development: Infants, children, adolescents, adults (6th ed.)*. Boston: McGraw-Hill College.

- Geuze, R.H., Jongmans, M.J., Schoemaker, M.M., & Smits-Engelsman, B.C.M. (Eds.) (2001). Developmental coordination disorder: Diagnosis, description, processes and treatment. In P.J. Beek & P.C.W. van Wieringen (Eds.), *Human Movement Science, 20*(1-2).

- Henderson, S.E. (Ed.) (1994). Developmental coordination disorder. In G. Reid (Ed.), *Adapted Physical Activity Quarterly, 11*(2).

- Kamps, P.H. (2000). *Modificability of the psychomotor domain*. Unpublished doctoral thesis, Calgary, AB, Canada: The University of Calgary.

- Kowalski, T.P. (2002). *The source for Asperger's syndrome*. East Moline, IL: LinguiSystems, Inc.

- Kranowitz, C.S. (1998). *The out of sync child: Recognizing and coping with sensory integration dysfunction*. New York: The Berkley Publishing Group.

- Reese, P.B., & Challenner, N.C. (1999). *Autism & PDD: Social skills lessons*. East Moline, IL: LinguiSystems, Inc.

- Reid, G. (Ed.) (1994). *Adapted Physical Activity Quarterly, 11*(2).

- Richard, G.J. (1997). *The source for autism*. East Moline, IL: LinguiSystems, Inc.

- Richard, G.J., & Hoge, D.R. (1999). *The source for syndromes 1*. East Moline, IL: LinguiSystems, Inc.

- Rourke, B.P. (1985). *Neuropsychology of learning disabilities*. New York: The Guilford Press.

- Rourke, B.P. (1987). Syndrome of nonverbal learning disabilities: The final common pathway of white-matter disease/dysfunction? *The Clinical Neuro-psychologist, 1*(3), 209-234.

- Rourke, B.P. (1989a). Nonverbal learning disabilities, socioemotional disturbance, and suicide: A reply to Fletcher, Kowalchuk and King, & Bigler. *Journal of Learning Disabilities, 22*(3), 186-187.

- Rourke, B.P. (1989b). *Nonverbal learning disabilities: The syndrome and the model.* New York: The Guilford Press.

- Rourke, B. (1998). Significance of verbal-performance discrepancies for subtypes of children with learning disabilities: Opportunities for the *WISC-III.* In A. Prifitera & D. Saklofske (Eds.), *WISC-III Clinical use and interpretation: Scientist-practitioner perspectives* (pp. 140-156). San Diego, CA: Academic Press.

- Rourke, B., & Fuerst, D.P. (1991). *Learning disabilities and psychosocial functioning: A neuropsychological perspective.* New York: The Guilford Press.

- Rourke, B., & Tsatsanis, K.D. (2000). Nonverbal learning disabilities and Asperger syndrome. In A. Klin, F.R. Volkmar, & S.S. Sparrow (Eds.), *Asperger syndrome* (pp. 231-251). New York: The Guilford Press.

- Rourke, B.P., Young, G.C., & Leenars, A.A. (1989). A childhood learning disability that predisposes those afflicted to adolescent and adult depression and suicide risk. *Journal of Learning Disabilities, 22*(3), 169-175.

- Smith Myles, B., & Simpson, R.L. (2001). Understanding the hidden curriculum: An essential social skill for children and youth with Asperger syndrome. *Intervention in School and Clinic, 36*(5), 279-286.

- Thompson, S. (1997). *The source for nonverbal learning disorders.* East Moline, IL: LinguiSystems, Inc.

- Trott, M.C., Laurel, M.K., & Windeck, S.L. (1993). *SenseAbilities: Sensory integration.* Tucson, AZ: Therapy Skill Builders.

Chapter Three

- Tsatsanis, K.D. (2005, April). Diagnostic boundaries and clinical characteristics: Autism, Asperger syndrome, and NLD. *Non-Verbal Learning Disabilities Conference.* Calgary, AB, Canada: The University of Calgary.

- Wechsler, D. (1991). *Wechsler intelligence scale for children (3rd ed.).* San Antonio, TX: The Psychological Corporation.

- Wechsler, D. (2003). *Wechsler intelligence scale for children (4th ed.).* San Antonio, TX: The Psychological Corporation.

- Whiting, H.T.A., & Whiting, M.G. (Eds.) (1998). *Human Movement Science, 17*(4-5).

- Wilbarger, P., & Wilbarger, J.L. (1991) *Sensory defensiveness in children aged 2-12: An intervention guide for parents and other caretakers.* Santa Barbara, CA: Avanti Educational Programs.

- Williams, K. (2001). Understanding the student with Asperger syndrome: Guidelines for teachers. *Intervention in School and Clinic, 36*(5), 259-265.

- Winders, P.C. (1997). *Gross motor skills in children with Down syndrome: A guide for parents and professionals.* Bethesda, MD: Woodbine House, Inc.

- Wing, L. (1981). Asperger's syndrome: A clinical account. *Psychological Medicine, 11*(1), 115-129.

- Wing, L. (1998). The history of Asperger's syndrome. In E. Schopler, G. Meisbov, & L.J. Kunce (Eds.), *Asperger's Syndrome or High Functioning autism?* (pp. 11-28). New York: Plenum Press.

- Winzer, M. (1990). *Children with exceptionalities: A Canadian perspective (2nd ed.).* Scarborough, ON, Canada: Prentice-Hall Canada Inc.

- World Health Organization (1996). *International classification of diseases (ICD): Multi-axial classification of child and adolescent psychiatric disorders (10th ed.).* Cambridge, UK: Cambridge University Press.

- Yack, E., Sutton, S., & Aquilla, P. (1998). *Building bridges through sensory integration.* Weston, ON, Canada: Print 3.

Chapter Four

Because poor motor coordination has the ability to significantly affect academic progress, home life, and eventual career choices, individuals with motor skill difficulties need and deserve help. After professionals have recognized the extent of a child's motor problems and a diagnosis has been made, the next step is to pursue appropriate intervention. It is hoped that treatment, therapy, and/or individual teaching will begin before secondary characteristics (e.g., anxiety, depression, or other issues) start affecting the child.

This chapter addresses various ways to improve children's motor skills in different environments. The following topics are included in this chapter:

1 Three Approaches to Motor Skill Training

The terms *bottom-up*, *top-down*, and *metacognitive* will be introduced and discussed in terms of approaches to motor skill training. Each approach has advantages and disadvantages, but the focus in this book will be on metacognition because it seems to best match the relative strengths of children with DCD. Remember, the diagnostic criteria for children with DCD described earlier assumes average to above-average intelligence. Most of the other disorders described in the previous chapter also assume typical cognitive development and abilities. Metacognitive strategies require students to analyze, think, reason, and be active in their learning. Intelligent children are able to explore, process, and purposefully examine how they learn, thereby strengthening and solidifying their abilities.

2 Questions to Consider Before Beginning Training

There are key questions that teachers, parents, and teacher's assistants should think about and answer before designing and beginning the training sessions with each student. The thoughtful answers to these questions, along with the careful analysis of each child's strengths, weaknesses, potential, and needs, will yield solid training practices.

3 General Recommendations for Parents/Caregivers

This section makes specific recommendations for parents and caregivers. The *how* and the *why* for each recommendation are also presented. Parents and caregivers are reminded to work closely with the school staff.

4 Strategies for School Professionals

Specific recommendations for the school environment are presented, along with explanations for the *how* and the *why* for each strategy.

5 Strategies Within the Community

Suggestions are given for the community, again discussing the *how* and the *why* for each recommendation.

6 Specific Teaching Strategies and Tips

Specific teaching strategies and tips will be reviewed for use in many settings, including the rationale for each technique.

You are not expected to try all the ideas with every student. The best advice is simply to start with a couple of the strategies and see how your child learns. If an approach works, continue using it. If the child requires some new teaching ideas (or you do!), try some different strategies.

Remember that, like most good teaching practices, many of these activities are not new or exceptionally creative ideas; you may well have already thought of and/or tried some of the methods presented. If so, the strategies that follow may simply confirm that you have been doing the right thing all along.

■ Three Approaches to Motor Skill Training

Unfortunately, because few children with DCD are currently diagnosed and since certain programs of therapy have not shown long-term gains, there are limited resources for parents, teachers, and classroom assistants to access for help. Over time, research findings help practitioners develop insight about how to help students with DCD improve their motor skills.

▶ The Bottom-Up Approach

Initially, rehabilitative exercises and "bottom-up" approaches were used to rectify motor difficulties. Intervention from this perspective is based on the idea that the child lacks information from sensory systems and basic motor abilities, so those domains need to be developed or strengthened before new motor learning can occur.

Chapter Four

The principles supporting a bottom-up approach are somewhat consistent with Piaget's theory of cognitive development. Piaget believed that without initial motor explorations and sensory experiences, a child acquired minimal learning during the sensorimotor period of development. This limitation consequently hindered higher order concept formation, abstract reasoning, and problem-solving abilities. Hence, this lack of experience needed to be addressed before any other training.

> A bottom-up approach is based on the idea that the child lacks information from sensory systems and basic motor abilities, so those domains need to be developed or strengthened before new motor learning can occur.

After an assessment of the sensory input systems that discloses the deficiencies in various motor skills, clinicians focus on changing areas of weakness by stimulating and promoting development of the sensory systems. They hope that over time and with continued support and intervention, the person will acquire the basic motor skills required for efficient movement and performance.

Although it would be very time consuming to implement this approach properly, some of these ideas are still valuable when working with children with coordination problems. After all, if children develop solid and efficient fundamental motor skills, they will be more successful as they continue learning and acquiring more specialized motor skills.

Unfortunately, a true bottom-up approach assumes that the child must master all underlying skills before performing higher-level skills or specialized motor actions. Assuming that the child never acquires the basic skills, she could be deprived of learning opportunities for skills she may actually be able to perform. Moreover, if the child is a passive participant in this approach and does not understand why she is asked to perform certain exercises and skills as part of her intervention program, she may not be very interested or motivated to continue learning simple skills in order to achieve a long-term goal far in the future.

▶ The Top-Down Approach

In contrast, the top-down approach seeks to help a child successfully perform functional skills in natural settings. For example, if a student wishes to learn to hit a baseball so he can join others during recess, the focus will be on acquiring or adjusting the different components of the task to make the learning effective. If the student is unable to perform the desired skill, several approaches can be implemented. A teacher or therapist may work toward improving the student's skills by descending down the skill hierarchy only to the point at which the student can be successful. The clinician can choose to modify or adjust tasks, change rules, or adjust environmental conditions so the student can be victorious in his learning.

A top-down approach seeks to help a child successfully perform functional skills in natural settings.

In the top-down approach, specific skills are targeted. Students are expected to work on motor activities that their classmates are learning, and they are not expected to spend time acquiring lower-level basic skills. The top-down approach, therefore, tends to be more motivating, interesting, and applicable to real-life situations.

Even with the best intervention and teaching, though, the child may not be able to perform the desired skill and, as a result, may experience failure and frustration. In addition, because of weaker general understanding about what the body can and is required to do (and how to react in different situations), there may be safety risks with this approach.

Finally, if the student has simply learned to perform a specific skill in a set environment, she may be unable to transfer or generalize the learned behaviors to another similar motor task.

▶ The Metacognitive Approach

In a metacognitive approach, the student is actively thinking about how and what he is to learn throughout the training process. The metacognitive approach is becoming well recognized as a valuable teaching and learning style for improving motor skills.

Chapter Four

Several writers explain that when adults passively manipulate or lead children through various motions, the neurological control of the movement is not the same as when the movement is actively undertaken by the learner. Children actually receive less data about the movement experience because only certain sensory receptors are functioning during passive actions. This limited input results in little, if any, motor information becoming available for learning. In contrast, some people report that the most important aspects of learning motor skills are these:

• To encourage and engage the thought processes of learners during motor experiences

• To facilitate learners to make their own decisions about various aspects of the educational process

• To assist the transfer of decision-making from the teacher to the learner in a progressive manner

Metacognition alone, though, may still not be the best solution for learning motor skills. Some professionals believe that the cognitive processes or mediating behavior children are led to focus on during learning experiences is actually more important than the short-term, practical motor performance outcomes. However, this approach alone does not address the emotional/social realm. A more interdisciplinary approach needs to be used because all learning requires processing and abilities in the verbal and nonverbal domains.

Fortunately, Bushner (1988) summarizes what appears to be the best method. Because of their interconnectedness, "effective teaching and learning must activate all three domains of learning (cognitive, affective, psychomotor)" (p. 53). This statement suggests that true motor learning involves physical performance coupled with cognitive functioning (as in planning through to the completed execution of a task) in a purposeful and desired manner because the student desires to learn the skill.

> Because of their interconnectedness, effective teaching and learning must activate the cognitive, affective, and psychomotor domains.

Chapter Four

How does one facilitate this type of learning? Through social constructivism. Here is a quick review of the theoretical basis of this approach.

Lev Vygotsky (1896-1934), a Russian psychologist, is credited with the idea of metacognition and/or cognitive education. In the 1930s, he developed a theory that describes how children acquire skills. He believed that information is transferred or passed from a competent person to a learner via mediation (interpsychological communication). Once the information is processed within (intrapsychological understanding), learning has occurred. In short, knowledge is *constructed* by *social interactions* with more competent others. According to many scholars, and summarized by Kamps (2000), this type of learning is promoted by active cognitive processes, such as the "reviewing, rethinking, reflecting, revisiting, and recognition of how experiences, ideas, and concepts become organized in meaningful ways" (p. 42).

> Social constructivism: knowledge is constructed by social interactions with more competent others (the process moves from interpsychological exchanges of information to intrapsychological processing).

Specifically related to motor skill acquisition, the metacognitive approach expects the person to be an active participant in the learning process. Each student should be asked to think about and analyze what happens during physical education and movement tasks, how he learns, and what aspects of movement and sports-related activities he needs altered in order to be more successful. In addition, the individual should be encouraged to continually think about how the new information can be applied to other situations, thus stimulating transfer and generalization of the new information. After all, the goal of learning is to apply new knowledge efficiently in established or novel situations as necessary.

The metacognitive approach seems particularly well suited to students with DCD and those with other motor learning disabilities because these children are of normal or above-average intelligence, and as such, it seems appropriate to use their skills in logic, reasoning, and concept formation to facilitate motor skill acquisition. In this book, *metacognition* is used to mean that the person is encouraged to think or analyze how she learns best.

Metacognition: the person is encouraged to think or analyze how she learns best

During the last few decades, the metacognitive approach has been used purposefully and very successfully in many teaching situations. Numerous researchers are now documenting study findings that show the benefits of this approach with learners. As a specific example, a group of research-oriented occupational therapists at McMaster University in Hamilton, Ontario, Canada, have been working on the development of a program that utilizes a metacognitive teaching format specifically for students with motor learning difficulties.

Because the children described in this book have average to above-average intelligence, it seems appropriate to use their skills in logic, reasoning, and thinking to facilitate motor skill acquisition.

■ Questions to Consider Before Beginning Training

The teaching strategies that follow have been used successfully when teaching children how to acquire basic gross motor skills as well as specific skills required in physical education classes and those that may be used within various recreational pursuits. Students learned these skills:

- running

- jumping

- balancing

- skipping

- ball skills (e.g., kicking, throwing, catching, bouncing, shooting)

- basic skills in badminton, basketball, baseball, floor hockey, soccer, football, and trampoline

Many of the students also learned to ride a scooter, a bicycle, or a skateboard. In addition, general principles of kinesthetic awareness, motor planning, full body/hand-eye coordination, and other speed and accuracy skills were taught.

Chapter Four

Fortunately, research and personal experience reveals that it is possible to reverse the clumsiness and physical awkwardness of many students who have difficulties with motor learning and performance. For example, after one or two 60-minute group sessions of specialized intervention, it was not uncommon to hear a ten-year old say, "I played baseball during recess last week. I also played yesterday because you showed me how to stand and hit the ball. I can play now!"

Although you may have specific skills that you want your student to learn, the best approach is to let the child have ownership in the decision-making process from the beginning. After she has the opportunity to participate this way and gains are made in her areas of interest, over time, she will likely be more accepting of other people's ideas and suggestions.

Nevertheless, parents, teachers, classroom assistants, and therapists need to ask themselves some tough questions before initiating training. Some key questions are listed below:

1   Will I be able to let the student set some personal goals, or do I need to set the main learning goals for this person?

2   Will I be able to alter the way I see "success" in the eyes of the child? With what level of proficiency will the student need to perform the skills before I will consider the performance successful?

3   Am I able to modify my lessons or teaching style to take this student's needs into account? If so, how should I do it?

4   Am I able to break the required skill into its component parts?

5   Will I rush the child's learning because it happens to come easier for me?

6   How will I be able to explain to the child that the task he wishes to learn may be too complex and unsafe? Will we be able to modify the goal enough so that the child will still desire to learn the skill and feel a measure of success?

7   Am I ready to provide the student with the metacognitive strategies she needs in order to learn? Can I model the verbal planning, processing, and purpose behind each explanation to the student as I teach?

8   How will my teaching style facilitate knowledge to the learner? How will I know the learning has occurred?

Chapter Four

As mentioned earlier, most of the following ideas are geared for learning gross motor skills. Fortunately there are many resources available to parents and teachers that deal specifically with fine motor tasks. Nevertheless, the basic principles in the following strategies will be beneficial when teaching any motor tasks.

■ General Recommendations for Parents/Caregivers

The following seven items are not truly teaching strategies; they are recommendations designed specifically for parents. Parents are and always will be a child's best advocate; hence your efforts will set the standard for what others can be expected to do for and with your child. If you do not actively pursue these suggestions, it will be difficult to expect teachers, coaches, therapists, or any others to follow through with additional teaching methods. If you do follow these recommendations, you will be able to explain to other people how and why some of the following concepts work well with your child.

1 Determine the cause of your child's motor difficulties so that you will know what you are dealing with.

> **Why:** If you understand that your child's motor problems are medically based, part of another condition that may be very difficult to change, or a DCD/motor learning disability, you will better understand how to address the condition and support your child.

> **How:** Schedule a regular medical check-up with your family doctor and explain any concerns about your child's motor behaviors, delays, and differences. Then seek out a more detailed assessment by a qualified professional who can give you the information you need to go further down the road of diagnosis. Find a clinician who can make the diagnosis of what is causing the motor difficulties or lead you to someone else who can. Is it developmental coordination disorder? If so, a medical doctor, with the support of a report by an occupational or physical therapist, will hopefully recognize the *DSM-IV-TR* condition that you are referring to. If your doctor does not know it, provide him with the data on page 92.

Chapter Four

2   If your child's motor problem is related to a motor learning disability such as DCD, share the pertinent information with your school's administrator and your child's homeroom, resource, and physical education teachers.

    Why: Educating yourself and others is a powerful way to spread information about your child's needs. The staff at your child's school may never have heard of DCD before, so they will not know how to deal with it. You can help fast-track their learning.

    How: Make all of these staff members aware of the assessment findings by providing them with a copy of the doctor's report or another document for the school files. Ensure that your child is recognized as having a learning disability. Furthermore, based on the regulations in your school district, your child may also qualify as having a medical or physical disability. In many settings, this will qualify your child as having a multiple disability.

3   Once your child is recognized as having a disability or learning need, the teachers at school will need to develop an Individualized Educational Plan (IEP) or Individualized Program Plan (IPP).

    Why: Your child is now recognized as having specific learning needs and the school is mandated to assist him in his need. If, for example, your son with DCD struggles with writing or needs more time to respond to questions, he has the legal right to receive those accommodations for state or provincial government exams. He should also have appropriate accommodations for other classroom work and assignments.

    How: The IEP or IPP document will identify the goals and strategies that will be used to facilitate the student's academic progress. It records how parents and teachers will adjust academic requirements, helps monitor your child's progress, and assists in planning future transitions. The goals and strategies used to help your child should be listed on the IEP/IPP. Before you sign this document, you should have a clear understanding and know what measures will be taken for and with your child to help him learn and improve his skills.

4   Explain the reality of the motor difficulties to teachers and other individuals who will work with your child. Describe how such difficulties impact functioning in other domains of behavior.

Chapter Four

Why: Until you learned about this topic or experienced it for yourself, it was probably a surprise to you about how all-encompassing motor difficulties can be. It affects much more than just the performance of motor skills. Teachers and other people who work with your child also may not know or have thought of the impact of motor difficulties on other aspects of life. Help them learn, because only then can they truly understand and help your child.

How: It is very easy to become emotionally affected when teachers question the fact that your child has difficulty learning motor skills. Teachers may react as if they do not believe you! As a result, you may find it particularly difficult to comment or respond to their questions the first few times.

Nevertheless, you will want them to learn about your child's difficulties. Consider purchasing a copy of this book for the school or compiling a list of journal articles or other resources for the school staff to review. That way, they can read about motor difficulties from a neutral source. They may feel the information is more credible if others also write about the topic, and they can see the immense amount of international research that has been generated on this topic. Teachers seldom receive resources from parents. They would likely be very impressed with your gift to them – and, out of respect to you, take time to learn about your child's condition – and, better yet, what to do about it.

To reduce the amount of reading for the staff or others, it may be very beneficial to place sticky notes or other markers in strategic locations in the book. Consider highlighting certain portions of the book to make it easier for the school staff members to review information quickly. They will certainly appreciate your efforts. If they choose to read more on their own, that's great. If not, they will have scanned the material you think is most valuable.

5 Educate yourself about the cause of your child's motor difficulties by reading various articles, books, and other resources related to this topic.

Why: You will gain more understanding about this topic and you may find other beneficial teaching strategies. You will also be more prepared to answer other people's questions, and it will assist you in becoming a strong advocate for your child's needs.

How: Go to the local library or ask the neighborhood bookstore to order books with titles about DCD, dyspraxia, etc. Then consider sharing the resources with other parents.

6 Consider establishing a parent-support group for other families who have children with DCD.

Why: There is compassion and understanding when you gather with other people who share similar difficulties. Other parents will acknowledge and comprehend the difficulties you have had to face with your child with DCD. In addition, many people can share the load to make a situation easier and they can make lighter work of certain situations. For example, other men and women may have already found clinicians, schools, therapists, or other service providers who know the cause of your child's struggles and what you need in the way of diagnostic terms and intervention. If so, you can save a great deal of time, energy, and possible frustration by learning from and sharing with each other.

How: Because of laws guarding privacy and the confidentiality of clients, you will not be able to acquire names or addresses from the service providers you meet. However, you can document your name, phone number, e-mail address, etc., and leave copies of this information with the doctor or therapist you have already met. That way they can give your information to similar individuals who are looking for additional support. You could also write a brief article in a local newspaper or magazine about child development. If you use words such as *uncoordinated*, *clumsy*, *awkward* or *klutzy* in the title, you will likely find the type of parents you are looking for. At the bottom of the article, include an invitation for parents to contact you if they have additional questions or wish to begin a support group, and then wait patiently. From there the information will start to spread slowly, but your group will grow over time.

7 Review what is being done to meet your child's needs within the school system on a regular basis. Remember to work _with_ the school staff in all stages of this process.

Why: You will want to stay abreast of what is happening at school every couple of weeks because you will be very upset if, after several months, you hear that your child is having major difficulties. Although you may assume that your child's teacher will contact you if troubles arise (and many will), the reality is that teachers are extremely busy and may have interruptions or other commitments when planning to communicate with you. If you contact them first, they will be more likely to return your calls.

It is also good to work closely with the school's teachers because they will be your allies at school in your absence. If the teachers feel challenged or threatened by your approach, they will have difficulty supporting and promoting your child's needs with other staff members.

How: Treat the teachers and administrators with respect and professionalism. Explain your child's needs and offer them background information in a simple and efficient manner. Encourage them with comments, and surprise them with a note or other small token of appreciation. They will work hard for your child if they feel you understand that they already have many other learning needs and issues to address within their respective classrooms.

Review what is being done to meet your child's needs within the school system on a regular basis. Work with the school staff in all stages of this process.

■ Strategies for School Professionals

You are likely a very busy professional who takes your work seriously and who is committed to educating each student you encounter. That's why you entered this career! You want all of your learners to acquire, refine, and apply skills and concepts they did not know before. You may also feel overwhelmed by your students' needs and the expectations placed upon you by your supervisors and the children's parents. I understand. I worked as a special education teacher for years.

Chapter Four

This section is not written to add extra work to your load; rather, it is offered to help you acquire some new teaching methods. Most of these are excellent ideas for pupils of all ages. I hope you will find them beneficial and a refreshing addition to your ever-growing toolbox of teaching ideas.

1   Alter the games and skills required in physical education, during sports-day functions and events, or in other recreational activities so that the playing field will be leveled for all participants.

Why: Children who have motor-learning problems usually recognize that they are less capable than others, and this becomes most noticeable during physical activities. These students do not want other people to notice that their skills are weak, so they often choose to sit out rather than join in. You can purposefully include them in activities by changing events to accommodate their learning needs and still have an enjoyable time with all participants.

How: Here are several examples:

a   Rather than having all individuals run a predetermined distance, allow students to run for a short time period and document how far each child traveled. Then multiply this amount by 10 or 20 as an expected distance covered. Next, encourage each student to run for the same time period and ask each of them to judge his or her own success in the activity.

b   If the required skill involves jumping over an object, string a rope or line from the ground to a higher point, creating a diagonal slope. Then allow students to jump across the rope at a point they feel comfortable with.

c   Rather than having all students participate primarily in sports events, ask students to divide into groups to create a "human sculpture." All individuals can brainstorm ideas, help to plan the eventual art form, and then hold or create a position that is part of the overall design. The student with motor learning problems will feel success and be an active participant in the event.

d   Review other ideas in books about adaptive physical education. These are wonderful resources full of many applicable ideas.

Chapter Four

2   Do not let skilled athletes choose teams in physical education.

Why: Too often the child with motor learning difficulties will be the last child chosen for teams. In addition, when team captains have to choose among the last few students, they often turn away and start to plan with the rest of their team. Then the teacher usually appoints the last few players among the teams. No one should have to face this embarrassment on a daily basis.

How: Encourage the division of all classmates for various physical education games and activities using classifications other than athletic skills or popularity ratings. For instance, pick teams according to shoe size, hair color, date of birth, the numbers of letters in one's first or last name, the number of pets they have in their families, the letters at the end of one's name, or the numbers in their addresses. Another alternative is to have students count off by the number of teams available.

3   The student with motor difficulties requires unrestricted access to all recess and outdoor play activities.

Why: Because the child with poor coordination needs as much opportunity for physical activity as possible.

How: Be especially careful not to keep the student inside for disciplinary measures during recess or lunch times, especially for tasks that he finds extremely difficult (e.g., redoing or completing writing or printing tasks). All students benefit from a movement break, and, in fact, they generally come back into class refreshed and more energized to learn. By withholding this time of physical exercise and enjoyment from the child with motor coordination problems, you are further impacting the student's difficulties and reducing the opportunities to learn to move and socialize with peers.

Furthermore, making a student stay indoors to perform a task that is genuinely difficult for the child reinforces the student's dislike of the task he does poorly. Say, for example, that you have great difficulty vacuuming or dusting, and someone else decides that, although you have free tickets to a great concert, you must stay home to practice vacuuming and dusting so you can get better at it. Do you think you would enjoy it more or get better at it as a result of staying home and doing those activities while your friends and neighbors get to go to the concert? I think not!

4 Give advance notice that you would like to observe the student's motor performance several minutes before you assess the child's quality of movement. Then do so discretely.

Why: A student with motor learning difficulties often takes longer to process and plan her physical response to a task. As such, she may feel anxious if asked to perform a movement task on the spot. The resultant performance would not approximate what the student really can do; it would only reveal what happens when she feels hurried and tense. You will not get a valid assessment.

How: Give the student a three- to five-minute warning of your need to view her skills. Then create a less threatening situation by asking the student to perform the task when all other students are still active in their own motor tasks, and/or position yourself so that the child with movement difficulties can show you the task in a less public location. You might even purposefully modify task requirements and assignments in ways that the awkward child can display a measure of success and possibly dare to show others her skills in public. If the student becomes successful and more confident over time and requests the opportunity to display her skills publicly, allow the opportunity. Then comment on the aspects of the motor skill that were successful, offer much praise, and encourage classmates to also celebrate the success with their peer.

5 Reduce the amount and complexity of the motor tasks that the uncoordinated student must produce.

Why: Although it is much more difficult for students with DCD to perform motor skills than other students, they still need to practice in order to learn. Therefore, encourage them to slow down. Simplify the task and focus on the quality of the motor performance instead of the speed.

How: Rather than having the child perform 25 basketball shots using poor form, for example, encourage him to think carefully about how the leg, arm, and shooting action should occur. If he only makes one or two baskets but uses proper form, modify your grading of the student's skills.

6 Teach the student with motor difficulties to ask questions or speak up in class when he does not understand a concept or skill.

Why: Since research has shown that many students with DCD have reasonably strong verbal skills, they should be able to use their area of relative strength for learning. Encourage these children to ask questions about the motor task. They, as well as other students, will receive additional information and/or clarification about the intended motor task. This is a good teaching technique for all children, not just those with motor learning difficulties.

How: Repeat instructions clearly and slowly. Ask the learner or another classmate to rephrase what she understood about the instructions. Then reinforce whether or not the student heard the instructions properly and, if necessary, clarify the directions.

7 Modify the way you assign a mark or grade for the uncoordinated child.

Why: When a student is found to have learning difficulties, the state or provincial government allows differing marking systems to be implemented for the student. Some schools will simply place a star or other symbol on the report card indicating that the student's mark has been modified and is not compared with other classmates.

How: If parents ask or you must assign some type of grade, first consider the child's baseline skills and then use this baseline as the criteria against which to measure success. Score progress in physical education and other motor-related tasks according to the learner's own advancement in skill performances. You could also overlook the uncoordinated student's quality of movement and grade the child based on his effort to produce the desired motor action to a level of personal proficiency.

8 Use collaborative teaching methods with the student who struggles with motor learning.

Why: Each learner has diverse reactions to the various teaching approaches and personalities of those who teach and work with him. If you can find out who and why someone may be more effective with the student than yourself (or if the child seems more engaged in learning with you), share your knowledge with others – not as a way to boast about your successes, but to share information of how best to instruct the student.

How: Take time to communicate with others who work and live with the student (e.g., teachers, coaches, parents, Scout leaders). Discuss what accommodations others have already made for the child and what they have discovered are the best learning modalities. Then use these successful techniques and stay in touch with others about their success stories as well.

9 Be prepared and willing to make allowances for the "klutzy" child's inability to learn motor skills in the same manner as his classmates.

Why: Each of us learns differently – some of us through verbal and/or auditory processing, some of us via visual modalities, and others by moving and/or kinesthetic approaches.

How: During the instructional phase of your lesson, provide varied teaching approaches for the entire class. This variety will help the child with motor learning problems and is also good teaching for all students. Even though you may not know each student's favored learning style, your students will likely gravitate to the method that best meets their unique needs.

At some point you could ask a particular student about his learning preferences so you can better tailor your instruction. Then, encourage your student to learn the parts of motor skills he is able to manage and provide positive reinforcement whenever he performs, transfers, or generalizes those skills to other physical activities.

> During the instructional phase of your lesson, provide varied teaching approaches for the entire class. This variety will help the child with motor learning problems and is also good teaching for all students.

■ Strategies Within the Community

This brief section addresses activities and events that occur outside of school hours (e.g., late afternoons, evenings, weekends). Although your child may be very tired after a full day at school, he will also benefit from additional opportunities for physical exercise and casual social contacts. Community activities allow for these to occur, often away from your child's classmates. Furthermore, when well planned, community events are also a very good way to create meaningful and quality time with your child away from the busy life at home.

1 Provide opportunities for your child to participate in single or small group physical activities that she wants to learn.

Why: Your child will be more self-motivated to participate and learn if she feels she has some input into decisions made about and for them.

How: Do some homework by investigating and then listing the types of activities you would support, can afford, and can arrange transportation for. Consider whether or not other gifted athletes or classmates will be at the same location. If so, you may wish to reconsider the decision to join the group, or be very open with your child about interacting with others who may ridicule her at some point. Then ask your child if there are any specific events from the list you created that she wishes to pursue.

If appropriate, accompany your child to the site a few times, and consider communicating your child's needs with the instructor before the event begins. If and when you decide to explain to the instructor that your child struggles with motor learning, offer two or three strategies that you know work exceptionally well and give some simple examples. Stay in touch with the instructor to see how your child is managing, but keep your contacts very brief. Ask your child how she is enjoying the scheduled activities.

2 Plan simple outings during weekends or evenings that will stimulate casual and enjoyable physical activity.

Why: The child with DCD is not naturally motivated to be active, so you may need to encourage opportunities for movement. Furthermore, by inviting the young person to join you for evening and weekend outings, you are purposefully modeling the importance of a physically active lifestyle. As an added bonus, it will permit you to have a short break from your day-to-day activities; you will have time to chat and enjoy each other's company, and you may find you also enjoy the opportunity to do something active and lively.

How: Schedule something very easy and functional the first few times. Here are some suggestions:

- Plan to walk or ride your bikes to the corner store to buy a newspaper.

- Walk the family dog together.

- Ask a neighbor if he would like help raking his lawn. Offer to rake along with your child.

- Invite your child to fly a kite with you or toss a ball in the park or watch some neighbors playing at the local tennis court.

- Bike a few blocks with your child to check out the new billboard or sign you saw on your way home from work today.

- Explore various kinds of construction projects happening nearby. If these things are not convenient from your doorstep, drive or take a bus somewhere before you walk.

- Plan a picnic with your child for supper in a local park.

- Try an overnight camping trip or visit a museum together.

- Watch the ducks in a pond, a river, or at a fountain downtown.

- Just try to make time to do these kinds of things several times a week. The list of ideas is endless!

3 Encourage your child to be involved in only one or two extra-curricular activities at a time.

Why: Because motor learning is more difficult for the child with DCD than for other children, it will require much concentration and effort to make gains. Furthermore, each child requires some down time at the end of each day to play, relax, and pursue activities he enjoys. The down time provides the child with a period of refreshment and recreation the same way that all of us like (and need) for our own interests and activities. Your child will be fresher for learning the next day.

How: For some parents who want their child to learn, do, be involved, have opportunities they never had, and in other ways "get ahead," it may be difficult to limit extracurricular activities for the child with motor difficulties. Over-commitment is not healthy for children or adults. Therefore, simply set limits for your child, who may actually be relieved to have some personal free time.

If your child feels pressured by others to do more, offer to take the flack yourself. For instance, instruct your child to tell others, "My mom (or dad) told me that I can only do _____, and that's why I can't _____." Your child will save face and peers should quickly stop bothering him.

Specific Teaching Strategies and Tips

Finally, here is what most of you are waiting for – the instructional techniques to use directly with the children.

Most of the suggestions apply to students across many settings. However, first and foremost, the student with DCD (or other motor learning problems) needs information broken down in ways that will help her learn more efficiently. Just as a pupil who has trouble reading or doing math skills needs intervention with more specific guidance than her classmates, the teacher, parent, or therapist usually starts by teaching the basics in a way that the child can grasp the concepts and move forward at her own rate of learning and understanding. Although there are always exceptions to the way students acquire skills, the reality is that most will need simple, clear, detailed instructions, and not too many instructions at once.

You may choose to use one or several of the following ideas at a time. That is fine; just stick with the ideas that work and do not present your learner with too many different strategies at a time lest the child feel like he is trying to juggle too many balls at once. You may also feel overwhelmed if you are consciously trying to remember and use more than two or three fundamental ideas.

The ideas that follow are not listed in any magical order, and one strategy is not better than another. Determine which idea(s) you think will best assist your child, student, or client, and then implement them.

Chapter Four

Chapter Four

As mentioned earlier, it is assumed that the learner will have some say in the skill(s) he is learning. The other assumption is that an adult or more proficient individual will be teaching the student. Also note that background data (lower-level skills, the rationale behind a strategy, and other such information) may need to be presented first. That said, the following strategies are offered for your consideration.

- Use task analysis to divide the desired motor task into small and easily manageable parts. (*Task analysis* requires you to analyze or break the task into its component bits.) Then, when the student has gained confidence and ability in several parts of the task, combine several components to begin a chained motor response. Continue to combine the various parts in the proper sequence until the child's motor performance approximates the required task.

  Do not be alarmed by the slow, jerky, and uncoordinated movements you may see initially. With continued planning and performance, the child should eventually display more fluid and controlled movements.

- Explain the basics of the required motor task. Start by describing the complete movement requirements. Then inform the learner of the components you want him to learn. In addition, explain why you want the child to gain those aspects of the skill. Then present the detailed information in the proper sequence.

- Demonstrate the required task very simply and directly, but do not assume that the student is already able to manage some or all of the underlying components of the task. You may need to pre-teach those components.

- Encourage the learner to listen to instructions and watch demonstrations with a purpose. For example, before providing instructions about a new motor skill, prompt with, "Listen and watch carefully. I want you to explain and show me the three main steps of this motor skill." Then confirm or clarify the student's understanding.

- Ask the pupil what strategies she thinks will be beneficial for her learning.

- Typically, you should teach by facing the student to be certain he sees and hears the information you present. However, upon occasion, it is important to stand with your back toward the learner so he can copy your motions exactly (e.g., you position your left foot and he positions his left foot in the same way, or you position your right arm and he positions his right arm in the same way).

Chapter Four

- Present information at a slower rate of speed than usual. Pause between instructions or explanations so the student has time to process and understand the task.

- Use slow, systematic, coordinated motions, and encourage the learner to imitate your movements or other people's movements.

- To teach about one's body position in space, provide opportunities for students to move in, around, under, through, etc., various objects and pieces of equipment. At first, encourage the child to speak out loud while moving through such obstacle courses or physical environments. Allow the child to monitor her own speed. As she becomes more proficient, ask her to consider moving faster and/or increase the difficulty of the tasks.

- When the student is learning a new skill, check for proper form. Then ask the student to consciously repeat the skill numerous times in order to start to develop motor memory.

- To help the student feel that he can master some motor related tasks, reduce the amount of motor-related information that you present. Provide only the basics about the fundamental skills you want the student to acquire.

- Teach motor skills by naming objects, limbs, and other body parts. In addition, use simple language to label specific motions and create slow-motion displays and other exaggerated demonstrations of the movement sequences you are teaching.

- Use diagrams, clear descriptions, or other teaching props when introducing new motor skills.

- Rather than simply showing the child what to do in one fast action, show and tell the learner the various components of the skill you want the student to learn. To do this, position your own body, a peer's body, or the child's body in a frozen pose.

- Help the learner understand how one movement is really much like other skills the child has done previously (e.g., raising one's arm in class is somewhat similar to the action required to throw balls and/or return an opponent's badminton birdie with an overhand drive with a badminton racquet). Use these associations as ways of grouping new motor skills with previously learned information.

Chapter Four

- When assessing how the student is managing motor tasks, provide the child with limited and specific feedback about the motor performances. Use basic terminology and offer additional recommendations about one or two aspects of the motor performance.

- If the child looks confused or frustrated, repeat the information and/or explain it to her in another manner.

- Facilitate effective learning for the auditory learner by talking the student through the various steps needed for the motor skill. After you model how an individual can use this strategy, encourage the child to use self-talk to stay focused and organized. Over time, ask the student to verbalize the steps quietly, saying them to himself (using inner speech) while performing the skill, until the action becomes automatic.

- Explain concepts related to size, force, weight, speed, and other such factors before the child needs to deal with it physically. Allow the student to gain a cognitive understanding of how to react to these various elements, and then encourage her to imagine or role-play her responses before a situation arises when she must participate physically.

- During the instructional portion of the lesson, explain various bio-mechanical principles and how they relate to different motor actions. This strategy is especially beneficial if the child is intelligent. Do not be afraid to use terms such as *levers*, *pendulums*, *spinning motions*, *rotation*, *center of gravity*, etc. Then be prepared to make some drawings, show pictures, or describe these principles clearly. For example, hip action while walking along a balance beam, delivering a curling rock, or releasing a bowling ball is similar to a pendulum swing.

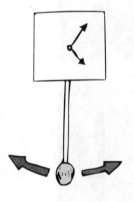

- Allow the learner to have sufficient time to organize his thoughts and actions in order to formulate a response. Although he may know and understand what he is supposed to do, he may be resistant to display the skill as quickly as you request to see it. In this case, allow the child to show you the skill privately when he is ready, or inform the student that you want to see him perform the activity at a specific time (and in another location) when other people and/or peers will not be watching.

- Determine whether the youth you are working with has acquired all the declarative and/or procedural knowledge required for the performance of fundamental motor skills you are trying to teach. (*Declarative knowledge* means that the child knows what to do and why, whereas *procedural knowledge* means that the student knows how to do the skill.) Always explain new concepts from the ground level upward.

- Encourage the child to visualize the desired motor response before producing it herself. Have her create a mental image of each step in the motor plan and clarify the proper sequence before trying it physically.

- Help the student analyze the direction of the planned movement. This strategy may help the brain pre-plan what messages to relay to the muscles before the action begins.

- Permit the student to use a 3-D model (e.g., a wooden mannequin, paper doll, or other such form) to help position and understand the various aspects of the motor activity. This way the learner can scrutinize the desired body position, attempt to recreate the pose with his own body, and eventually try performing the task (e.g., when learning to walk along a narrow balance beam, position the arms outward to assist with balance).

- Help the child find another activity she can currently perform that is somewhat similar to the required or desired task. For example, when walking up steps, one foot is momentarily balancing your body. This momentary one-foot balance also occurs when kicking a ball.

  Encourage the student to consciously associate various similar activities together for later recall. If this is too difficult for the student to think of or recall at first, provide her with appropriate motor associations.

- Encourage the learner to ask other students how they plan their motor activities. Have the student watch his peers in action so he knows what the required task looks like. Alternatively, perform certain motor activities in front of a mirror so the student can see the results of his motor planning in action.

- Affirm the anxiety that the student will likely feel about having to perform a new or difficult motor task. Remind the child that it will be very challenging to perform the skill in the same manner every time, but that it is important to try her best so that motor skills will become easier in the future. (Remind the student that she does not likely think about lifting each leg and placing it in a certain spot when walking anymore.) Assure the learner that over time, she will likely produce her motor movements just as automatically.

- Explain to the child that the purpose of learning motor patterns efficiently is so that the brain does not need to spend extra cognitive energy on performing the task. The brain can focus instead on different parts of the motor activity (e.g., how fast the ball is coming and which way one needs to move to catch it).

For example, encourage the student to participate in a simple, repetitive motor activity (e.g., riding a stationary bicycle or raising a hand and forearm up and down). After he has performed the skill for some time and appears proficient at it, ask him questions while he continues to perform the activity. This strategy may help the learner understand the concept of performing a motor pattern automatically, even though his brain is processing and responding to other information.

- Encourage the child to think about her plan – to move consistently and in the same manner with each performance. Provide direct instruction about proceeding slowly and carefully during initial trials of a task.

- Reinforce the need to perform motor skills in the same manner over and over. You may even choose to mark specific spots on the floor where the student should place his feet when trying specific skills for the first few times (e.g., when preparing to position the feet in relation to the home plate when preparing to bat a ball in baseball). Alternatively, you may stand beside the child the first few times that he performs a skill so that he can see exactly how to position a limb or his body most efficiently (e.g., using a baseball glove for catching).

- Encourage the student to simply ask you for further clarification of the task if she does not understand what is expected.

Chapter Four

- Use visual cues such as a picture series or a sequence of individuals performing the required skill. Tape these onto the wall of the gymnasium, the garage door, the wall of your home, or other similar location. If the child seems more receptive to written directions, provide written explanations of each step underneath the individual pictures.

  The steps/stages involved in motor learning are often found in good physical education manuals. If you do not have access to such information, ask the physical education teacher or a physical therapist to find such information for you. Enlarge the pictures so it will be easier for the learner to see. If there are specific aspects of the skill that are somewhat difficult, circle that spot on the picture to bring attention to that feature of the movement skill.

- Provide the learner with as much review and repetition as needed in order to execute the motor task successfully.

- Capitalize on the child's strengths in the cognitive domain to assist motor skill acquisition. For example, encourage him to follow a four-step formula when trying to perform all physical activities. This simple procedure may increase the student's cognitive understanding of the psychological processes involved in motor activity, and, in this way, help the learner gain a clearer understanding of what is involved in each task.

  1. Set a GOAL.
  2. Make a PLAN for how to perform the skill.
  3. DO the activity.
  4. CHECK how it went. Then repeat, adjust, or set a new GOAL.

- Use posters, teaching sheets, or other strategies to help the student recall the GOAL, PLAN, DO, CHECK formula. Use these terms freely during teaching times, and ask the student frequently which of the four steps she is currently processing.

Chapter Four

■ Summary

This chapter offered information about theories and practical applications of methods to boost students' motor learning. Initially, three different approaches to motor skill intervention were identified. A very brief summary as well as the pros and cons of *bottom-up*, *top-down*, and *metacognitive* approaches were presented. Another concept, *social constructivism*, was also used to help explain the metacognitive approach to teaching.

Then, eight questions were presented as a way to help adults, parents, therapists, or teachers analyze their own expectations and perceptions before working with the learner. This set of questions was followed by detailed descriptions of teaching strategies or recommendations for helping the child with motor learning problems. Parents, as their child's strongest advocate, were challenged to follow the recommendations listed under their section. Teachers were encouraged to view the teaching strategies for students with motor disorders not as additional work, but as new, refreshing ideas to add to their toolbox of teaching tricks.

Next, several ideas for community involvement outside of school hours were presented. Finally, more than 30 teaching strategies to use directly with your learners were offered.

It is hoped that you will find some or all of these methods applicable and helpful for working with children with motor disorders. If nothing else, this information may simply confirm that you are using the right strategies already!

■ References

- Barnhill, G.P. (2001). What is Asperger's syndrome? *Intervention in School and Clinic, 36*(5), 259-265.

- Benbow, M. (2002). Hand skills and handwriting. In S.A. Cermak & D. Larkin (Eds.), *Developmental coordination disorder,* (pp. 247-279). Clifton Park, NY: Thompson Delmar Learning.

- Burton, A.W., & Miller, D.E. (1998). *Movement skill assessment.* Champaign, IL: Human Kinetics Publishers, Inc.

- Bushner, C.A. (1988). Can we help children move and think critically? In W.J. Stintson (Ed.), *Moving and learning for the young child (pp. 51-66).* Reston, VA: American Alliance for Health, Physical Education, Recreation & Dance (AAHPERD).

- CAHPERD (1994). *Moving to inclusion - Active living through physical education: Maximizing opportunities for students who are physically awkward.* Ottawa, ON, Canada: Canadian Association for Health, Physical Education, Recreation & Dance (CAHPERD).

- Cheatum, B.A., & Hammond, A.A. (2000). *Physical activities for improving children's learning and behavior: A guide to sensory motor development.* Champaign, IL: Human Kinetics Publishers, Inc.

- Cratty, B.J. (1989). *Adapted physical education in the mainstream (2nd ed.).* Englewood Cliffs, NJ: Prentice-Hall, Inc.

- French, K.E., & Nevett, M.E. (1993). Knowledge representation and decision-making in sport. In G.E. Stelmach, P.A. Vroon (Series Ed.), J.L. Starkes, & F. Allard, (Vol. Eds.), *Advances in Psychology: Cognitive issues in motor expertise* (Vol. 102) (pp. 255-270).

- Gallahue, D.L., & Donnelly, F.C. (2003). *Developmental physical education for all children.* Champaign, IL: Human Kinetics Publishers, Inc.

- Haywood, K.M. (1986). *Life span motor development.* Champaign, IL: Human Kinetics Publishers, Inc.

- Henderson, S.E., & Sugden, D.A. (1992). *Movement assessment battery for children.* London: The Psychological Corporation, Ltd.

Chapter Four

- Kamps, P.H. (2004). Developmental coordination disorder. *Advance for Speech-Language Pathologists and Audiologists, 14,* 12.

- Keogh, J.F., & Sugden, D.A. (1985). *Movement skill development.* New York: Macmillan Publishers.

- Kimball, J.G. (2002). Developmental coordination disorder from a sensory integration perspective. In S.A. Cermak & D. Larkin (Eds.), *Developmental coordination disorder, (*pp. 210-220). Clifton Park, NY: Thompson Delmar Learning.

- Kirby, A. (1999). *Dyspraxia: The hidden handicap.* Guernsey, Great Britain: The Guernsey Press Co., Ltd.

- Kirchner, G., & Fishburne, G.J. (1998). *Physical education for elementary children (10th ed.).* Boston: WCB/McGraw-Hill.

- Kurtz, L.A. (2004). *How to help a clumsy child: Strategies for young children with developmental motor concerns.* London: Atheneum Press, Gateshead, Tyne and Wear.

- Larkin, D., & Parker, H.E. (2002). Task-specific intervention for children with developmental coordination disorder: A systems view. In S.A. Cermak & D. Larkin (Eds.), *Developmental coordination disorder,* (pp. 234-247). Clifton Park, NY: Thompson Delmar Learning.

- Levine, M.D. (1981). *The answer system: School questionnaire* (Form 1S). Recreation & Dance: Educators Publishing Service, Inc.

- May-Benson, T., Ingolia, P., & Koomar, J. (2002). Accommodations to functional settings for children with developmental coordination disorder. In S.A. Cermak & D. Larkin (Eds.), *Developmental coordination disorder, (*pp. 280-284). Clifton Park, NY: Thompson Delmar Learning.

- McPherson, S. (1993). Knowledge representation and decision-making in sport. In G.E. Stelmach, P.A. Vroon (Series Eds.), J.L. Starkes, & F. Allard (Vol. Eds.), *Advances in Psychology: Cognitive issues in motor expertise* (Vol. 102) (pp. 159-188).

- Missiuna, C. (Ed.) (2001). *Children with developmental coordination disorder: Strategies for success.* Binghamton, NY: Haworth Press, Inc.

- Missiuna, C., & Mandich, A. (2002). Integrating motor learning theories into practice. In S.A. Cermak & D. Larkin (Eds.), *Developmental coordination disorder,* (pp. 221-233). Clifton Park, NY: Thompson Delmar Learning.

- Mosston, M. (1968). *Teaching physical education.* Belmont, CA: Wadsworth.

- Mosston, M. (1972). *From command to discovery.* Minneapolis, MN: Burgess Publishing Company.

- Mosston, M., & Ashworth, S. (1994). *Teaching physical education (4th ed.).* New York: Macmillan College Publishing Company.

- Piaget, J. (1993). *The origins of intelligence* (M. Cook, Trans.). New York: W.W. Norton & Company, Inc. (Original work published in 1952).

- Portwood, M. (1999). *Developmental dyspraxia: Identification and intervention: A manual for parents and professionals (2nd ed.).* London: David Fulton Publishers.

- Reid, G. (Ed.). *Adapted Physical Activity Quarterly, 11*(2).

- Richard, G.J. (2000). *The source for treatment methodologies in autism.* East Moline, IL: LinguiSystems, Inc.

- Rink, J.E. (1996) Tactical and skill approaches to teaching sport and games: Introduction. *Journal of Teaching in Physical Education, 15,* 399-400.

- Rink, J.E., French, K.E., & Graham, K.C. (1996). Implications for practice and research. *Journal of Teaching in Physical Education, 15,* 490-508.

- Rink, J.E., French, K.E., & Tjeerdsma, B.L. (1996). Foundations for the learning and instruction of sport and games. *Journal of Teaching in Physical Education, 15,* 401-417.

- Ripley, K., Daines, B., & Barrett, J. (2003). *Dyspraxia: A guide for teachers and parents.* London: David Fulton Publishers.

- Schmidt, R.A. (1991). *Motor learning & performance: From principles to practice.* Champaign, IL: Human Kinetics Publishers, Inc.

Chapter Four

- Whiting, H.T.A., and Whiting, M.G. (Eds.) (1998). *Human Movement Science, 17.*

- Vygotsky, L.S. (1956). Learning and mental development at school age. In A.N. Leontiev & A.R. Luria (Eds.), *Selected psychological works* (written in 1938). Chapter provided in EDPS 693.14, Calgary, AB, Canada: The University of Calgary.

- Vygotsky, L.S. (1978). *Mind in society: The development of higher order psychological processes* (M. Cole, V. John-Steiner, S. Scribner, & E. Souberman, Eds. & Trans.) (Original works published 1930-1935). Cambridge, MA: Harvard University Press.

Chapter Five

Because this book deals with motor difficulties, this final chapter will begin with some very strong quotes related to the topic. Some general comments and concluding statements follow; these are especially for parents and caregivers for children with DCD.

- "Perhaps each school should have a staff member who knows how to look at a child with educational or behavior problems . . . by taking motor skills into account" (McKinlay quoted in the foreword of Russell 1988).

- "Research has demonstrated that motor problems in children can be very distressing and have significant long-term consequences; studies have found that children with DCD [or other significant difficulties with motor coordination] display poor social competency, have more academic and behavior problems, and have low self-esteem" (Crawford, Wilson, and Dewey 2001, p. 30).

- "The 'clumsy' child who progresses through school without any difficulty is the exception rather than the rule. Much more common are children whose lack of coordination is accompanied by lack of confidence, low self-esteem, under achievement in school, and loneliness" (Henderson and Sugden 1992).

At first glance these quotes may seem overly negative because they do not suggest any hope for students with DCD. However, the reality is that students with motor difficulties are being identified and helped more frequently now than in years past. The research on this group of students is clear; they need and deserve help. Fortunately, armed with new knowledge and insights, you can be instrumental in educating others about DCD. You may be a change agent providing teachers, therapists, and/or children with the strategies and ideas they need to help others. You may be instrumental in assisting people directly to acquire necessary skills and abilities in the motor domain; a large but awesome responsibility, and one to take seriously but also with joy.

After you first come to know that your child has DCD (or any other condition, for that matter), you may feel relieved. Your unease truly had a basis and you will feel validated that you really had a reason to be concerned. However, the next moment you may feel absolutely overwhelmed and not know where to turn or what to do next. Fortunately, things have a way of working themselves out, and after a few days, life will carry on much the same as before. In fact, it is not wise to allow such a diagnosis to become all-encompassing. Your life will quickly lose balance and order if you focus on a single issue for a long time.

Chapter Five

Although you may be tempted to spend a great deal of time and energy helping your child to acquire skills in the motor domain, take care of yourself and other members of your family. Do not jeopardize the health and well-being of your entire family over the issues that one child has. Your spouse (if applicable), close friends, and/or other children also need to feel that you are spending valuable time and energy with each of them too.

Search for professionals who understand your particular situation and who are in a position to support and counsel you in future decisions about your child. Do not be surprised if these individuals are difficult to access. If you find that they have exceptional clinical skills, others will probably feel the same about them, and these professionals will likely be overbooked and overworked. Regardless, stay in contact with doctors, therapists, and others who know and sense your needs and whom you trust and value.

Choose realistic interventions and/or therapy programs for your son or daughter. Carefully decide what types of sacrifices you are able and willing to make for your child's overall gain, but consider how these choices may impact other members of the family. The best option is to find activities and programs that will provide functional and maximum gain for the time and financial resources you put into them.

In addition, try to incorporate your child's needs and interventions into your day-to-day activities. That may necessitate a slight lifestyle change for many of you, but it is likely one worth making. After all, it may be beneficial to invite your entire family to go outdoors or in other ways engage in some physical activity. Nevertheless, several weeks after initiating such changes, take time to reassess and reconsider whether you wish to continue with this intervention model or consider making a change that may be even more beneficial.

Consider joining a support group that will help you during your time of questioning, investigating, and exploring. Then be willing to share what you learned with others who are just joining the group in search of their own answers. In Chapter Four, there is a short section on how to establish a support group (p. 138).

Beware of information that you access on this topic. In particular, be cautious about information you read on the Internet. It is very easy for someone to create a web page, write an article about her own experiences, and then post her page on the Internet without any other background information. A good measure of the value of any Internet article is to view the research listed at the end of the

Chapter Five

presentation. Is there any such reference list? Is the data generated primarily by one or a few select individuals? Are there similar articles, studies, and/or results from elsewhere in the world? Are the books and journals credible resources that are refereed by peers?

Although I am passionate about the importance of the impact of DCD on a child, I also understand that there are other more important ways to view the child with motor learning difficulties. Each of us has been given special skills and abilities, so rather than focusing primarily on your child's deficits, help him develop his exceptional qualities. Celebrate his talents and proficiencies in other areas. All people have a need to belong and feel validated; their relative strengths must be highlighted and celebrated within secure family settings and other supportive networks. If you focus primarily on your child's areas of difficulty, he may begin to feel even more awkward and different than he felt before you had a specific diagnosis.

While you are celebrating your child's strengths and interests, enjoy your opportunity to raise this child, bringing out his best for others to see and benefit from in the future.

Finally, remember to save some time and energy to deal with issues that are bigger and much more challenging and distressing than your child's motor difficulties. This larger-than-life philosophy will teach your child that he is very important, yet other things and issues in life matter, too. It's good modeling as your child transitions into adolescence16 and adulthood.

It has been an honor and privilege to be one of the first clinicians to write a practical resource about DCD – one that may eventually help some of these children as they journey through life. I hope that the information in this book is clear, easy to understand, but most of all helpful as you tell and teach others what you have learned. It is my sincere wish that you will now take your newly acquired knowledge and share and apply it when helping other people. As a helper of people, your intrapersonal response makes for a full and fruitful life of service to others, especially the child with motor coordination difficulties.

Chapter Five

■ References

- Crawford, S.G., Wilson, B.N., & Dewey, D. (2001). Identifying developmental coordination disorder: Consistency between tests. In C. Missiuna (Ed.), *Children with developmental coordination disorder: Strategies for success* (p. 29-50). Binghamton, NY: The Haworth Press, Inc.

- Henderson, S.E., & Sugden, D.A. (1992). *Movement assessment battery for children.* London: The Psychological Corporation, Ltd.

- Russell, J.P. (1988). *Graded activities for children with motor difficulties.* Foreword by I. McKinlay, Consultant Pediatric Neurologist, University of Manchester School of Medicine. Musselburgh, Scotland: Cambridge University Press.

References

- Adreon, D., & Stella, J. (2001). Transition to middle and high school: Increasing the success of students with Asperger syndrome. *Intervention in School and Clinic, 36*(5), 266-271.

- Ahonen, T. (1990). Developmental coordination disorders in children: A developmental neuropsychological follow-up study. *Jyvaskyla Studies in Education, Psychology & Social Research, 78.*

- American Psychiatric Association (1987). *Diagnostic and statistical manual of mental disorders (3rd ed. revised)*. Washington, DC: Author.

- American Psychiatric Association (1994). *Diagnostic and statistical manual of mental disorders (4th ed.)*. Washington, DC: Author.

- American Psychiatric Association (2000). *Diagnostic and statistical manual of mental disorders (4th ed. – text revision)*. Washington, DC: Author.

- Attwood, T. (1998). *Asperger's syndrome: A guide for parents and professionals.* London: Jessica Kingsley Publishers.

- Attwood, T. (2000, Nov. 15). Effective strategies to aid social/emotional development for more able individuals with Autism and Asperger's syndrome. Calgary, AB, Canada: Presentation sponsored by Geneva Centre for Autism.

- Ayres, A.J. (1979). *Sensory integration and the child.* Los Angeles, CA: Western Psychological Services.

- Ayres, A.J. (1980). *Sensory integration and learning disorders.* Los Angeles, CA: Western Psychological Corporation.

- Ayers, A.J. (1985). *Developmental dyspraxia and adult onset apraxia.* Torrance, CA: Sensory Integration International.

- Ayres, A.J., Mailloux, Z.K., & Wendler, C.L.W. (1987). Developmental dyspraxia: Is it a unitary function? *Occupational Therapy Journal of Research, 7*(2), 93-110.

- Barnett, A., & Henderson, S.E. (1992). Some observations on the figure drawings of clumsy children. *British Journal of Educational Psychology, 62,* 341-355.

• Barnett, A.L., Kooistra, L., & Henderson, S.E. (Eds.) (1998). *Clumsiness as syndrome and symptom.* In H.T.A. Whiting & M.G. Whiting (Eds.), *Human Movement Science, 17*(4-5).

• Barnhill, G.P. (2001). What is Asperger's syndrome? *Intervention in School and Clinic, 36*(5), 259-265.

• Baumgardner, T., & Reiss, A.L. (1994). Fragile X syndrome: A behavioral genetics' window into understanding social emotional learning disability. In A.J. Capute, P.J. Accardo, & B.K. Shapiro (Eds.), *Learning disabilities spectrum: ADD, ADHD, & LD* (pp. 67-68). Timonium, Maryland: York Press, Inc.

• Bayley, N. (1993). *Bayley scales of infant development (2nd ed.).* San Antonio, TX: Therapy Skill Builders.

• Beek, P.J., & van Wieringen, P.C.W. (Eds.) (2001). *Human Movement Science, 20*(1-2).

• Benbow, M. (1995). Principles and practices of teaching handwriting. In A. Henderson & C. Pehoski (Eds.), *Hand function in the child* (pp. 255-281). St. Louis, MO: Mosby Publishing.

• Benbow, M. (2002). Hand skills and handwriting. In S.A. Cermak & D. Larkin (Eds.), *Developmental coordination disorder* (pp. 247-279). Clifton Park, NY: Thompson Delmar Learning.

• Bigler, E.D. (1989). On the neuropsychology of suicide. *Journal of Learning Disabilities, 22*(3), 180-185.

• Bock, M.A. (2001). SODA strategy: Enhancing the social interaction skills of youngsters with Asperger syndrome. *Intervention in School and Clinic, 36*(5), 272-278.

• Bouffard, M., Watkinson, E.J., Thompson, L.P., Causgrove-Dunn, J.L., & Romanow, S.K.E. (1996). A test of the activity deficit hypothesis with children with movement difficulties. *Adapted Physical Activity Quarterly, 13,* 61-73.

• Brenner, M.W., & Gillman, S. (1966). Visuo-motor ability in school children: A survey. *Developmental Medicine and Child Neurology, 8,* 686-703.

- Brownell, M.T., & Walther-Thomas, C. (2001). Steven Shore: Understanding the autism spectrum: What teachers need to know. *Intervention in School and Clinic, 36*(5), 293-299, 305.

- Bruininks, R.H. (1978). *Bruininks-Oseretsky test of motor proficiency.* Circle Pines, MN: American Guidance Service.

- Bruner, J. (1973). Organization of early skilled action. *Child Development, 44*(1), 1-11. In D.L. Gallahue & J.C. Ozman (Eds.), *Understanding motor development: Infants, children, adolescents, adults (3rd ed.).* Dubuque, IA: WCB Brown & Benchmark Publishers.

- Bryan, T. (1998). Social competence of students with learning disabilities. In B.Y.L. Wong (Ed.), *Learning about learning disabilities (2nd ed.)* (pp. 237-275). Toronto, ON, Canada: Academic Press.

- Burton, A.W., & Miller, D.E. (1998). *Movement skill assessment.* Champaign, IL: Human Kinetics Publishers, Inc.

- Bushner, C.A. (1988). Can we help children move and think critically? In W.J. Stintson (Ed.), *Moving and learning for the young child* (pp. 51-66). Reston, VA: American Alliance for Health, Physical Education, Recreation & Dance (AAHPERD).

- CAHPERD (1994). *Moving to inclusion: Active living through physical education: Maximizing opportunities for students who are physically awkward.* Ottawa, ON: Canadian Association for Health, Physical Education, Recreation & Dance (CAHPERD).

- Cantell, M. (1998). Developmental coordination disorder in adolescence: Perceptual motor, academic and social outcomes of early motor delay. *Research Reports on Sport & Health, 112.*

- Cantell, M., & Kooistra, L. (2002). Long term outcomes of developmental coordination disorder. In S.A. Cermak, & D. Larkin (Eds.), *Developmental coordination disorder* (pp. 23-38). Clifton Park, NY: Thompson Delmar Learning.

- Cantell, M.H., Smyth, M.M., & Ahonen, T.P. (1994). Social and affective problems of children who are clumsy: How early do they begin? In S.E. Henderson (Ed.), *Developmental coordination disorder.* In G. Reid (Ed.), *Adapted Physical Activity Quarterly, 11*(2), 115-129.

165

- Case-Smith, J., & Weintraub, N. (2002). *Hand function and developmental coordination disorder.* In S.A. Cermak & D. Larkin (Eds.), *Developmental coordination disorder* (pp. 157-171). Clifton Park, NY: Thompson Delmar Learning.

- Causgrove-Dunn, J., & Watkinson, E.J. (1994). A study of the relationship between physical awkwardness and children's perceptions of physical competence. *Adapted Physical Activity Quarterly, 11*, 274-283.

- Causgrove-Dunn, J., & Watkinson, E.J. (2002). Considering motivation theory in the study of developmental coordination disorder. In S.A. Chermak & D. Larkin (Eds.), *Developmental coordination disorder* (pp. 185-199). Clifton Park, NY: Thompson Delmar Learning.

- Cermak, S. (1991). Somatodyspraxia. In A.G. Fisher, E.A. Murray, & A.C. Bundy (Eds.), Developmental neuropsychology and soft neurological signs: An update. Special issue of *Developmental Neuropsychology.*

- Cermak, S. (1991). Somatodyspraxia. In A.G. Fisher, E.A. Murray, & A.C. Bundy (Eds.), *Sensory integration: Theory and practice* (pp. 137-165). Philadelphia, PA: F.A. Davis Company.

- Cermak, S.A., Gubbay, S.S., & Larkin, D. (2002). What is developmental coordination disorder? In S.A. Cermak & D. Larkin (Eds.), *Developmental coordination disorder* (pp. 2-22). Clifton Park, NY: Thompson Delmar Learning.

- Cermak, S.A., & Larkin, D. (Eds.) (2002). *Developmental coordination disorder.* Clifton Park, NY: Thompson Delmar Learning.

- Cermak S.A., & Larkin, D. (2002). *Families as partners.* In S.A. Cermak & D. Larkin (Eds.), *Developmental coordination disorder* (pp. 200-208). Clifton Park, NY: Thompson Delmar Learning.

- Cheatum, B.A., & Hammond, A.A. (2000). *Physical activities for improving children's learning and behavior: A guide to sensory motor development.* Champaign, IL: Human Kinetics Publishers, Inc.

- Clements, S.D. (1966). Minimal brain dysfunction in children: Terminology and identification. *NINBD Monograph 3.* Washington, DC: U.S. Government.

- Coleman, R., Piek, J.P., & Livesey, D.J. (1998). *A longitudinal study of motor ability and kinesthetic acuity in young children at risk of developmental coordination disorder.* In P.J. Beek & P.C.W. van Wieringen (Eds.), *Human Movement Science, 20*(1-2), 95-110.

- Cornoldi, C., Rigoni, F., Tressoldi, P.E., & Vio, C. (1999). Imagery Deficits in nonverbal learning disabilities. *Journal of Learning Disabilities, 32*(1), 48-57.

- Cratty, B.J. (1989). *Adapted physical education in the mainstream (2nd ed.).* Englewood Cliffs, NJ: Prentice-Hall, Inc.

- Crawford, S.G., Wilson, B.N., & Dewey, D. (2001). Identifying developmental coordination disorder: Consistency between tests. In C. Missiuna (Ed.), *Children with developmental coordination disorder: Strategies for success* (pp. 29-50). Binghamton, NY: Haworth Press, Inc.

- De Ajuriaguerra, J., & Stambak, M. (1969). Developmental dyspraxia and psychomotor disorders. In P.J. Vinken & G.W. Bruyn (Eds.), *Handbook of clinical neurology: Disorders of speech perception and symbolic behavior* (Vol. 4) (pp. 443-464).

- Dewey, D. (2000, October 6). Personal communication: Calgary, AB, Canada.

- Dewey, D. (2002). Subtypes of developmental coordination disorder. In S.A. Cermak & D. Larkin (Eds.), *Developmental coordination disorder* (pp. 40-53). Clifton Park, NY: Thompson Delmar Learning.

- Dewey, D., & Wilson, B.N. (2001). Developmental coordination disorder: What is it? In C. Missiuna (Ed.), *Children with developmental coordination disorder: Strategies for success* (pp. 5-27). Binghamton, NY: Haworth Press, Inc.

- Dimitrovsky, L., Spector, H., Levy-Shiff, R., & Vakil, E. (1998). Interpretation of facial expressions of affect in children with learning disabilities with verbal or nonverbal deficits. *Journal of Learning Disabilities, 31*(3), 289-292, 312.

- Drillien, C., & Drummond, M. (1983). Developmental screening and the child with special needs: A population study of 5000 children. *Clinics in Developmental Medicine,* No. 86.

- Duke, M.P., Nowicki, S. Jr., & Martin, E.A. (1996). *Teaching your child the language of social success.* Atlanta, Georgia: Peachtree Publishers, Ltd.

- Dupre (1911) (as cited in F.R. Ford, 1966). *Diseases of the nervous system in infancy, childhood & adolescence (5ᵗʰ ed.).* Thomas Springfield (HMS vol. 17).

- Dwyer, C., & McKenzie, B.E. (1994). Impairment of visual memory in children who are clumsy. In S.E. Henderson (Ed.), *Developmental coordination disorder.* In G. Reid (Ed.), *Adapted Physical Activity Quarterly, 11*(2), 179-189.

- Estil, L.B., & Whiting, H.T.A. (2002). Motor/language impairment syndromes: Direct or indirect foundations? In S.A. Cermak & D. Larkin (Eds.), *Developmental coordination disorder* (pp. 54-68). Clifton Park, NY: Thompson Delmar Learning.

- Fletcher, J.M. (1989). Nonverbal learning disabilities and suicide: Classification leads to prevention. *Journal of Learning Disabilities, 22*(3), 176, 179.

- Folio, M.R., & Fewell, R.R. (1983). *Peabody developmental motor scales and activity cards.* Austin, TX: PRO-ED.

- Foss, J.M. (1991). Nonverbal learning disabilities and remedial interventions. *Annals of Dyslexia, 41,* 128-140.

- Foss, J.M. (2000). Students with nonverbal learning disabilities. *NLD on the Web.* http://www.nldontheweb.org/foss.htm

- Fox, A.M., & Lent, B. (1996). Clumsy children: Primer on developmental coordination disorder. *Canadian Family Physician, 42,* 1965-1971.

- Frankenburg, W.K., & Dodds, J.B. (1967). *The Denver developmental screening test.* Denver, CO: University of Colorado Medical Center.

- Frankenberger, C. (2000). Nonverbal learning disabilities: An emerging profile. http://www.nldontheweb.org/frankenberger.htm

- French, K.E., & Nevett, M.E. (1993). Knowledge representation and decision-making in sport. In G.E. Stelmach, P.A. Vroon (Series Ed.), J.L. Starkes, & F. Allard (Vol. Eds.), *Advances in Psychology: Cognitive issues in motor expertise* (Vol. 102) (pp. 255-270).

- Gallahue, D.L., & Donnelly, F.C. (2003). *Developmental physical education for all children.* Champaign, IL: Human Kinetics Publishers, Inc.

- Gallahue, D.L., & Ozman, J.C. (2005). *Understanding motor development: Infants, children, adolescents, adults (6th ed.).* Boston: McGraw-Hill College.

- Gesell, A. (1925). *The mental growth of the preschool child: A psychological outline of normal development from birth to the sixth year, including a system of developmental diagnosis.* New York: Macmillan Publishers.

- Gesell, A., & Amatruda, C.S. (1941). *Developmental diagnosis: The evaluation and management of normal and abnormal neuropsychological development in infant and early childhood.* New York: P.B. Hoeber, Inc.

- Geuze, R.H., Jongmans, M.J., Schoemaker, M.M., & Smits-Engelsman, B.C.M. (Eds.) (2001). *Clinical and research diagnostic criteria for developmental coordination disorder: A review and discussion.* In P.J. Beek & P.C.W. van Wieringen (Eds.), *Human Movement Science, 20*(1-2), 7-47.

- Geuze, R.H., Jongmans, M.J., Schoemaker, M.M., & Smits-Engelsman, B.C.M. (Eds.) (2001). Developmental coordination disorder: Diagnosis, description, processes and treatment. In P.J. Beek & P.C.W. van Wieringen (Eds.), *Human Movement Science, 20*(1-2).

- Geuze, R.H., & Kalverboer, A.F. (1987). Inconsistency and adaptation in timing of clumsy children. *Journal of Human Movement Studies, 13,* 421-432.

- Geuze, R.H., & Kalverboer, A.F. (1994). Tapping a rhythm: A problem of timing for children who are clumsy and dyslexic? In S.E. Henderson (Ed.), *Developmental coordination disorder.* In G. Reid (Ed.), *Adapted Physical Activity Quarterly, 11*(2), 203-213.

- Geuze, R.H., & van Dellen, T. (1990). Auditory precue processing during a movement sequence in clumsy children. *Journal of Human Movement Studies, 19,* 11-24.

- Gillberg, I.C., & Gillberg, C. (1989). Children with preschool minor neurodevelopmental disorders: Behavior and school achievement at age 13. *Developmental Medicine and Child Neurology, 31,* 14-24.

- Gubbay, S.S. (1975). *The clumsy child: A study in developmental paraxial and agnostic ataxia.* London: W.B. Saunders.

- Hall, D. (1988). Clumsy children. *British Medical Journal, 296,* 375-376.

- Hands, B., & Larkin, D. (2002). Physical fitness and developmental coordination disorder. In S.A. Cermak & D. Larkin (Eds.), *Developmental coordination disorder* (pp. 172-184). Clifton Park, NY: Thompson Delmar Learning.

- Hay, J. (1992). Adequacy in and predilection for physical activity in children. *Clinical Journal of Sport Medicine, 2,* 192-201.

- Hay, J., & Missiuna, C. (1998). Motor proficiency in children reporting low levels of participation in physical activity. *Canadian Journal of Occupational Therapy, 65*(2), 64-71.

- Haywood, K.M. (1986). *Life span motor development.* Champaign, IL: Human Kinetics Publishers, Inc.

- Haywood, K.M., & Getchell, N. (2004). *Life span motor development (4th ed.).* Champaign, IL: Human Kinetics Publishers, Inc.

- Heller, W. (2000). Understanding nonverbal learning disability (NVLD). *http://www.nldontheweb.org/heller.htm*

- Hellgren, L., Gillberg, I.C., Bagenholm, A., Gillberg, C. (1994). Children with deficits in attention, motor control, and perception (DAMP) almost grown up; Psychiatric and personality disorders at age 16 years. *Journal of Child Psychology and Psychiatry, 35,* 1255-1271.

- Henderson, S., May, M., & Umney, D.S. (1989). An exploratory study of goal-setting behavior, self-concept and locus of control in children with movement difficulties. *European Journal of Special Needs Education, 4*(1), 1-15.

- Henderson, S.E. (Ed.) (1994). *Developmental coordination disorder.* In G. Reid (Ed.), *Adapted Physical Activity Quarterly, 11*(2).

- Henderson, S.E., & Barnett, A.L. (1998). *The classification of specific motor coordination disorders in children: Some problems to be solved.* In A.L. Barnett, L. Kooistra, & S.E. Henderson (Eds.), *Clumsiness as syndrome and symptom.* In H.T.A. Whiting & M.G. Whiting (Eds.), *Human Movement Science, 17*(4-5), 449-469.

- Henderson, S.E., Barnett, A., & Henderson, L. (1994). Visuospatial difficulties and clumsiness: On the interpretation of conjoined deficits. *Journal of Child Psychology & Psychiatry, 35,* 961-969.

- Henderson, S.E., & Hall, D. (1982). Concomitants of clumsiness in young school children. *Developmental Medicine and Child Neurology, 24,* 448-460.

- Henderson, S.E., & Sugden, D.A. (1992). *Movement assessment battery for children.* London: The Psychological Corporation, Ltd.

- Henderson, L., Rose, P., & Henderson, S. (1992). Reaction time and movement time in children with developmental coordination disorder. *Journal of Child Psychology and Psychiatry, 33,* 895-905.

- Hill, E.L., Bishop, D.V.M., & Nimmo-Smith, I. (1998). Representational gestures in developmental coordination disorder and specific language impairment: Error-types and reliability ratings. In A.L. Barnett, L. Kooistra, & S.E. Henderson (Eds.), *Clumsiness as syndrome and symptom.* In H.T.A. Whiting & M.G. Whiting (Eds.), *Human Movement Science, 17*(4-5), 655-678.

- Hoare, D. (1991). *Classification of movement dysfunctions in children: Descriptive and statistical approaches.* Unpublished doctoral dissertation, Nedlands, Western Australia: The University of Western Australia.

- Hoare, D. (1994). Subtypes of developmental coordination disorder. In S.E. Henderson (Ed.), *Developmental coordination disorder.* In G. Reid (Ed.), *Adapted Physical Activity Quarterly, 11*(2), 158-169.

- Hulme, C., Smart, A., & Moran, G. (1982). Visual perceptual deficits in clumsy children. *Neuropsychologia, 20,* 475- 481.

- Hulme, C., Smart, A., Moran, G., & Raine, A. (1983). Visual, kinesthetic and cross-modal development: Relationship to motor skill development. *Perception, 12,* 477- 483.

References

- Johnson, D.J., & Myklebust, H.R. (1967). *Learning disabilities: Educational principles and practices.* New York: Grune & Stratton, Inc.

- Kamps, P.H. (2000). *Modificability of the psychomotor domain.* Unpublished doctoral thesis, Calgary, AB, Canada: The University of Calgary.

- Kamps, P.H. (2004). Developmental coordination disorder. *Advance for Speech-Language Pathologists and Audiologists, 14,* 12.

- Kaplan, B.J., Wilson, B.N., Dewey, D., & Crawford, S.G. (1998). DCD may not be a discrete disorder. In A.L. Barnett, L. Kooistra, & S.E. Henderson (Eds.), *Clumsiness as syndrome and symptom.* In H.T.A. Whiting & M.G. Whiting (Eds.), *Human Movement Science, 17*(4-5), 471-490.

- Keogh, J. (1977). The study of movement skill development. *Quest, 28,* 76-88.

- Keogh, J.F., & Sugden, D.A. (1985). *Movement skill development.* New York: Macmillan Publishers.

- Kimball, J.G. (2002). Developmental coordination disorder from a sensory integrative perspective. In S.A. Cermak & D. Larkin (Eds.), *Developmental coordination disorder* (pp. 210-220). Clifton Park, NY: Thompson Delmar Learning.

- Kirby, A. (1999). *Dyspraxia: The hidden handicap.* Guernsey, Great Britain: The Guernsey Press Co., Ltd.

- Kirchner, G., & Fishburne, G.J. (1998). *Physical education for elementary children (10th ed.).* Boston, MA: WCB/McGraw-Hill.

- Knuckey, N.W., Apsimon, T.T., & Gubbay, S.S. (1983). Computerized axial topography in clumsy children with developmental paraxial and agnosia. *Brain and Development, 5*(1), 14-20.

- Kong, E. (1963). Minimal cerebral palsy: The importance of its recognition. In M. Bax & R. MacKeith (Eds.), Minimal cerebral dysfunction. *Little Club Clinics in Developmental Medicine, 10,* 29-31.

- Kowalchuk, B., & King, J. D. (1989). Adult suicide versus coping with nonverbal learning disorder. *Journal of Learning Disabilities, 22*(3), 177-179.

- Kowalski, T.P. (2002). *The source for Asperger's syndrome.* East Moline, IL: LinguiSystems, Inc.

- Kranowitz, C.S. (1998). *The out of sync child: Recognizing and coping with sensory integration dysfunction.* New York: The Berkley Publishing Group.

- Kurtz, L.A. (2004). *How to help a clumsy child: Strategies for young children with developmental motor concerns.* London: Atheneum Press, Gateshead, Tyne and Wear.

- Langaas, T., Mon-Williams, M., Wann, P., Pascal, E., & Thompson, C. (1998). Eye movements, prematurity and developmental co-ordination disorder. *Vision Research, 38,* 1817-1826.

- Larkin, D., & Cermak, S.A. (2002). *Issues in identification and assessment of developmental coordination disorder.* In S.A. Cermak & D. Larkin (Eds.), *Developmental coordination disorder* (pp. 86-102). Clifton Park, NY: Thompson Delmar Learning.

- Larkin, D., & Parker, H. (1997, May). *Physical self-perceptions of adolescents with a history of developmental co-ordination disorder.* Poster presentation at NASPSPA, Denver, CO.

- Larkin, D., & Parker, H.E. (2002). Task-specific intervention for children with developmental coordination disorder: A systems view. In S.A. Cermak & D. Larkin (Eds.), *Developmental coordination disorder* (pp. 234-247). Clifton Park, NY: Thompson Delmar Learning.

- Leew, J. (2001). Passport to learning: A cognitive intervention for children with organizational difficulties. In C. Missiuna (Ed.), *Children with developmental coordination disorder: Strategies for success* (pp. 145-159). Binghamton, NY: Haworth Press, Inc.

- Le Normand, M.T., Vaivre-Douret, L., Payan, C., & Cohen, H. (2000). Neuromotor development and language processing in developmental dyspraxia: A follow-up case study. *Journal of Clinical and Experimental Neuropsychology, (22)*3, 408-417.

References

- Levine, M.D. (1981). *The ANSER system: School questionnaire* (Form 1S). Cambridge, MA: Educators Publishing Service, Inc.

- Lippitt, L.C. (1926). *A manual of corrective gymnastics.* New York: Macmillan Publishers.

- Little, S.S. (1993). Nonverbal learning disabilities and socio-emotional functioning: A review of recent literature. *Journal of Learning Disabilities, 26*(10), 653-665.

- Lord, R., & Hulme, C. (1987). Perceptual judgments of normal and clumsy children. *Developmental Medicine and Child Neurology, 29,* 250-257.

- Losse, A., Henderson, S.E., Elliman, D., Hall, D., Knight, E., & Jongmans, M. (1991). Clumsiness in children: Do they grow out of it? A 10-year follow-up study. *Developmental Medicine and Child Neurology, 33,* 55-68.

- Lundy-Ekman, L., Ivry, R., Keele, S.W., & Woollacott, M. (1991). Timing and force control deficits in clumsy children. *Journal of Cognitive Neuroscience, 3,* 367-376.

- Macnab, J.J., Miller, L.T., & Polatajko, H.J. (1994). The search for sub-types of DCD: Is cluster analysis the answer? In P.J. Beek & P.C.W. van Wieringen (Eds.), *Human Movement Science, 20*(1-2), 49-72.

- Mandich, A.D., Polatajko, H.P., Macnab, J., & Miller, L.T. (2001). Treatment of children with developmental coordination disorder: What is the evidence? In C. Missiuna (Ed.), *Children with developmental coordination disorder: Strategies for success* (pp. 51-68). Binghamton, NY: Haworth Press, Inc.

- Mandich, A.D., Polatajko, H.J., Missiuna, C., Miller, L.T. (2001). In C. Missiuna (Ed.), *Children with developmental coordination disorder: Strategies for success* (pp. 125-143). Binghamton, NY: Haworth Press, Inc.

- May-Benson, T., Ingolia, P., & Koomar, J. (2002). Accommodations to functional settings for children with developmental coordination disorder. In S.A. Cermak & D. Larkin (Eds.), *Developmental coordination disorder* (pp. 280-284). Clifton Park, NY: Thompson Delmar Learning.

• May-Benson, T., Ingolia, P., & Koomar, J. (2002). Daily living skills and developmental coordination disorder. In S.A. Cermak & D. Larkin (Eds.), *Developmental coordination disorder* (pp. 140-156). Clifton Park, NY: Thompson Delmar Learning.

• McCabe, P., Rosenthal, J.B., & McLeod, S. (1998). Features of developmental dyspraxia in the general speech-impaired population. *Clinical Linguistics & Phonetics, 12*(2), 105.

• McConaughy, S.H., & Ritter, D.R. (1999). Psychological perspectives on exceptionality. In V.L. Schwean & D.H. Saklofske (Eds.), *Handbook of psychosocial characteristics of exceptional children* (pp. 41-68). New York: Kluwer Academic/Plenum Publishers.

• McGowan, T. (Ed.) (1994). Active living through physical education: Maximizing opportunities for students who are physically awkward. *Moving to Inclusion.* Gloucester, ON, Canada: Canadian Association for Health, Physical Education, Recreation & Dance (CAHPERD).

• McHale, K., & Cermak, S.A. (1992). Fine motor activities in elementary school: Preliminary findings and provisional implications for children with fine motor problems. *American Journal of Occupational Therapy, 46,* 898-903.

• McKinney, J.D. (1989). Longitudinal research on the behavioral characteristics of children with learning disabilities. *Journal of Learning Disabilities, 22*(33), 141-150. In McKinney, J.D., & Speece, D.L. (Eds.) (1986), Classification and validation of behavioral subtypes of learning-disabled children. *Journal of Educational Psychology, 7*(1), 67-77.

• McPherson, S. (1993). Knowledge representation and decision-making in sport. In G.E. Stelmach, P.A. Vroon (Series Eds.), J.L. Starkes, & F. Allard (Vol. Eds.), *Advances in Psychology: Cognitive issues in motor expertise* (Vol. 102) (pp. 159-188).

• Miller, L.T., Polatajko, H.J., Missiuna, C., Mandich, A.D., & Macnab, J.J. (2001). A pilot trial of a cognitive treatment for children with developmental coordination disorder. In P.J. Beek & P.C.W. van Wieringen (Eds.), *Human Movement Science, 20*(1-2), 7-47.

- Missiuna, C. (1994). Motor skill acquisition in children with developmental coordination disorder. In Henderson, S.E. (Ed.), *Developmental coordination disorder.* In G. Reid (Ed.), *Adapted Physical Activity Quarterly, 11*(2), 214-235.

- Missiuna, C. (1998). Development of "All About Me," a scale that measures children's perceived motor competence. *The Occupational Therapy Journal of Research, 18*(2), 85-108.

- Missiuna, C. (Ed.). (2001). *Children with developmental coordination disorder: Strategies for success.* Binghamton, NY: Haworth Press, Inc.

- Missiuna, C., Gaines, B.R., & Pollock, N. (2002). Recognizing and referring children at risk for developmental coordination disorder: Role of speech language pathologist. *Journal of Speech-Language Pathology and Audiology, (26)*4, 170-177.

- Missiuna, C., & Mandich, A. (2002). Integrating motor learning theories into practice. In S.A. Cermak & D. Larkin (Eds.), *Developmental coordination disorder* (pp. 221-233). Clifton Park, NY: Thompson Delmar Learning.

- Missiuna, C., Mandich, A.D., Miller, L.T., & Macnab, J.J. (2002). *Cognitive orientation to daily occupational performance (CO-OP): Part II - The evidence.* In C. Missiuna (Ed.), *Children with developmental coordination disorder: Strategies for success* (pp. 83-106). Binghamton, NY: Haworth Press, Inc.

- Missiuna, C., Mandich, A.D., Polatajko, H.J., & Malloy-Miller, T. (2002). Cognitive orientation to daily occupational performance (CO-OP): Part I- Theoretical foundations. In C. Missiuna (Ed.), *Children with developmental coordination disorder: Strategies for success* (pp. 69-81). Binghamton, NY: Haworth Press, Inc.

- Miyahara, M., Tsujii, M., Hanai, T., Jongmans, M., Barnett, A., Henderson, S.E., et al. (1998). The Movement Assessment Battery for Children: A preliminary investigation of its usefulness in Japan. In A.L. Barnett, L. Kooistra, & S.E. Henderson (Eds.), *Clumsiness as syndrome and symptom.* In H.T.A. Whiting & M.G. Whiting (Eds.), *Human Movement Science, 17*(4-5), 679-697.

- Mon-Williams, M.A., Pascal, E., & Wann, J.P. (1994). Ophthalmic factors in developmental coordination disorder. In S.E. Henderson (Ed.), *Developmental coordination disorder.* In G. Reid (Ed.), *Adapted Physical Activity Quarterly, 11*(2), 170-178.

- Moran, J.M., & Kalakian, L.H. (1977). *Movement experiences for the mentally retarded or emotionally disturbed child (2ⁿᵈ ed.).* Minneapolis, MN: Burgess Publishing Company.

- Morrison, S.R., & Siegel, L.S. (1991). Arithmetic disability: Theoretical considerations and empirical evidence for this subtype. In L.V. Feagins, E.J. Short, & L.J. Meltzer (Eds.), *Subtypes of learning disabilities: Theoretical perspectives & research* (pp. 189-208). Hillsdale, NJ: Lawrence Erlbaum Associates, Inc.

- Mosston, M. (1968). *Teaching physical education.* Belmont, CA: Wadsworth.

- Mosston, M. (1972). *From command to discovery.* Minneapolis, MN: Burgess Publishing Company.

- Mosston, M., and Ashworth, S. (1994). *Teaching physical education (4ᵗʰ ed.).* New York: Macmillan College Publishing Company.

- Murphy, F.D. (1983). *The acceptance and/or rejection patterns of LD children and their NLD peers in a mainstream setting.* Doctoral Dissertation, The University of Cincinnati. Ann Arbor, MI: University Microfilms International.

- Murray, E.A., Cermak, S.A., & O'Brien, V. (1990). The relationship between form and space perception, constructional abilities, and clumsiness in children. *American Journal of Occupational Therapy, 44,* 623-628.

- O'Beirne, C.O., Larkin, D., & Cable, T. (1994). Coordination problems and anaerobic performance in children. In S.E. Henderson (Ed.), *Developmental coordination disorder.* In G. Reid (Ed.), *Adapted Physical Activity Quarterly, 11*(2), 141-149.

- Orton, S.T. (1937). *Reading, writing and speech problems in children.* New York: W.W. Norton & Company, Inc.

References

- Ozols, E.J., & Rourke, B.P. (1985). Dimensions of social sensitivity in two types of learning-disabled children. In B.P. Rourke (Ed.), *Neuropsychology of learning disabilities: Essentials of subtype analysis* (pp. 281-301). New York: The Guilford Press.

- Parush, S., Yochman, A., Cohen, D., & Gershon, E. (1998). Relation of visual perception and visual-motor integration for clumsy children. *Perceptual and Motor Skills, 86,* 291-295.

- Piaget, J. (1993). *The origins of intelligence* (M. Cook, Trans.). New York: W.W. Norton & Company, Inc. (Original work published in 1952).

- Piek, J.P., & Coleman-Carman, R. (1995). Kinesthetic sensitivity and motor performance of children with developmental coordination disorder. *Developmental Medicine and Child Neurology, 37,* 976-984.

- Piek, J.P., & Skinner, R.A. (1999). Timing and force control during a sequential tapping task in children with and without motor coordination problems. *Journal of the International Neuropsychological Society, 5,* 320-329.

- Polatajko, H.J., Fox, A.M., & Missiuna, C. (1985). An international consensus on children with developmental coordination disorder. *Canadian Journal of Occupational Therapy, 62*(1), 3-6.

- Polatajko, H.J., Mandich, A.D., Missiuna, C., Miller, L.T., Macnab, J.J., Malloy-Miller T., & Kinsella, E.A. (2002). Cognitive orientation to daily occupational performance (CO-OP): Part III: The protocol in brief. In C. Missiuna (Ed.), *Children with developmental coordination disorder: Strategies for success* (pp. 107-123). Binghamton, NY: Haworth Press, Inc.

- Portwood, M. (1999). *Developmental dyspraxia: Identification and intervention: A manual for parents and professionals (2nd ed.).* London: David Fulton Publishers.

- Primeau, L. (1992). *Game playing behavior in children with developmental dysphasia.* Unpublished Master's Dissertation. Los Angeles, CA: University of Southern California.

- Psychologists Association of Alberta (2000, Oct. 28). Psychologists Working in Schools. Workshop presented in Calgary, AB, Canada.

- Rarick, G.L. (1961). *Motor development during infancy and childhood (Rev. ed.)*. Madison, WI: College Printing and Typing.

- Reese, P.B., & Challenner, N.C. (1999). *Autism & PDD: Social skills lessons*. East Moline, IL: LinguiSystems, Inc.

- Reid, G. (Ed.) (1994). *Adapted Physical Activity Quarterly, 11*(2).

- Rice, F.P. (1995). *Human development: A lifespan approach (2nd ed.)*. Englewood Cliffs, NJ: Prentice-Hall, Inc.

- Richard, G.J. (1997). *The source for autism*. East Moline, IL: LinguiSystems, Inc.

- Richard, G.J. (2000). *The source for treatment methodologies in autism*. East Moline, IL: LinguiSystems, Inc.

- Richard, G.J. (2001). *The source for processing disorders*. East Moline, IL: LinguiSystems, Inc.

- Richard, G.J., & Hoge, D.R. (1999). *The source for syndromes 1*. East Moline, IL: LinguiSystems, Inc.

- Richard, G.J., & Russell, J.L. (2001). *The source for ADD/ADHD*. East Moline, IL: LinguiSystems, Inc.

- Rink, J.E. (1996) Tactical and skill approaches to teaching sport and games: Introduction. *Journal of Teaching in Physical Education, 15*, 399-400.

- Rink, J.E., French, K.E., & Graham, K.C. (1996). Implications for practice and research. *Journal of Teaching in Physical Education, 15*, 490-508.

- Rink, J.E., French, K.E., & Tjeerdsma, B.L. (1996). Foundations for the learning and instruction of sport and games. *Journal of Teaching in Physical Education, 15*, 401-417.

- Rintala, P., Pienimaki, K., Ahonen, T., Cantell, M., & Kooistra, L. (1998). The effects of a psychomotor training programme on motor skill development in children with developmental language disorders. In A.L. Barnett, L. Kooistra, & S.E. Henderson (Eds.), *Clumsiness as syndrome and symptom*. In H.T.A. Whiting & M.G. Whiting (Eds.), *Human Movement Science, 17*(4-5), 721-737.

- Ripley, K., Daines, B., & Barrett, J. (2003). *Dyspraxia: A guide for teachers and parents*. London: David Fulton Publishers.

- Rosblad, B. (2002). Visual perception in children with developmental coordination disorder. In S.A. Cermak & D. Larkin (Eds.), *Developmental coordination disorder* (pp. 104-116). Clifton Park, NY: Thompson Delmar Learning.

- Rosblad, B., & Gard, L. (1998). The assessment of children with developmental coordination disorders in Sweden: A preliminary investigation of the Movement ABC. In A.L. Barnett, L. Kooistra, & S.E. Henderson (Eds.), *Clumsiness as syndrome and symptom*. In H.T.A. Whiting & M.G. Whiting (Eds.), *Human Movement Science, 17*(4-5), 711-709.

- Rosblad, B., & von Hofsten, C. (1994). Repetitive goal-directed arm movements in children with developmental coordination disorders: Role of visual information. In S.E. Henderson (Ed.), *Developmental coordination disorder*. In G. Reid (Ed.), *Adapted Physical Activity Quarterly, 11*(2), 190-202.

- Rose, B., Larkin, D., & Berger, B. (1997). Coordination and gender influences on the perceived competence of children. *Adapted Physical Activity Quarterly, 14,* 210-221.

- Rourke, B.P. (1985). *Neuropsychology of learning disabilities*. New York: The Guilford Press.

- Rourke, B.P. (1987). Syndrome of nonverbal learning disabilities: The final common pathway of white-matter disease/dysfunction? *The Clinical Neuropsychologist, 1*(3), 209-234.

- Rourke, B.P. (1989a). Nonverbal learning disabilities, socioemotional disturbance, and suicide: A reply to Fletcher, Kowalchuk and King, and Bigler. *Journal of Learning Disabilities, 22*(3), 186-187.

- Rourke, B.P. (1989b). *Nonverbal learning disabilities: The syndrome and the model*. New York: The Guilford Press.

- Rourke, B. (1998). Significance of verbal-performance discrepancies for subtypes of children with learning disabilities: Opportunities for the WISC-III. In A. Prifitera & D. Saklofske (Eds.), *WISC-III Clinical use and interpretation: Scientist-practitioner perspectives* (pp. 140-156). San Diego, CA: Academic Press.

- Rourke, B., & Fuerst, D.P. (1991). *Learning disabilities and psychosocial functioning: A neuropsychological perspective.* New York: The Guilford Press.

- Rourke, B., & Tsatsanis, K.D. (2000). Nonverbal learning disabilities and Asperger syndrome. In A. Klin, F.R. Volkmar, & S.S. Sparrow (Eds.), *Asperger syndrome* (pp. 231-251). New York: The Guilford Press.

- Rourke, B.P., Young, G.C., & Leenars, A.A. (1989). A childhood learning disability that predisposes those afflicted to adolescent and adult depression and suicide risk. *Journal of Learning Disabilities, 22*(3), 169-175.

- Russell, J.P. (1988). *Graded activities for children with motor difficulties.* Foreword by I. McKinlay, Consultant Pediatric Neurologist, University of Manchester School of Medicine. Musselburgh, Scotland: Cambridge University Press.

- Schmidt, R.A. (1991). *Motor learning & performance: From principles to practice.* Champaign, IL: Human Kinetics Publishers, Inc.

- Schoemaker, M.M., & Kalverboer, A.F. (1994). Clumsiness in adolescence: Educational, motor, and social outcomes of motor delay detected at 5 years. In S.E. Henderson (Ed.), *Developmental coordination disorder.* In G. Reid (Ed.), *Adapted Physical Activity Quarterly, 11*(2), 130-140.

- Schoemaker, M.M., & Kalverboer, A.F. (1994). Social and affective problems of children who are clumsy: How early do they begin? *Adapted Physical Activity Quarterly, 11*, 130-140.

- Schoemaker. M.M., van der Wees, M., Flapper, B., Verheij-Jansen, N., Scholten-Jaegers, S., & Geuze, R.H. (2001). Perceptual skills of children with developmental coordination disorder. In P.J. Beek & P.C.W. van Wieringen (Eds.), *Human Movement Science, 20*(1-2), 111-133.

- Scholten, T. (1999). *Attention deluxe dimension: A wholistic approach to ADD.* Calgary, AB, Canada: Manuscript Edition.

- Shafer, S.Q., Shaffer, D., O'Connor, P.A., & Stokman, C.J. (1986). Hard thoughts on neurological soft signs (pp. 133-143). In M. Rutter (Ed.), *Developmental neuropsychiatry.* Cambridge, UK: Cambridge University Press.

- Shaw, L., Levine, M.D., & Belfer, M. (1982). Developmental double jeopardy: A study of clumsiness and self-esteem in children with learning problems. *Developmental and Behavioral Pediatrics, 3*(4), 191-196.

- Sherrill, C. (1977). *Adapted physical education and recreation: A multi-disciplinary approach.* Dubuque, IA: Wm. C. Brown Company Publishers.

- Sherrill, C. (1993). *Adapted physical activity, recreation, and sport: Crossdisciplinary and lifespan (4ᵗʰ ed.).* Dubuque, IA: Wm. C. Brown Company Publishers.

- Short, H., & Crawford, J. (1984, February). Last to be chosen: The awkward child. *Pivot, 2,* 32-36.

- Siegel, L.S. (1989a). IQ is irrelevant to the definition of learning disabilities. *Journal of Learning Disabilities, 22*(8), 469-479.

- Siegel, L.S. (1989b). Why we do not need intelligence test scores in the definition and analysis of learning disabilities. *Journal of Learning Disabilities, 22*(8), 514-518.

- Siegel, L.S. (1999). Issues in the definition and diagnosis of learning disabilities: A perspective on Guckenberger v. Boston University. *Journal of Learning Disabilities, 32*(4), 304-319.

- Sigmundsson, H., & Whiting, H.T.A. (2002). Neural constraints on motor behavior in children with hand-eye coordination problems. In S.A. Cermak & D. Larkin (Eds.), *Developmental coordination disorder* (pp. 69-84). Clifton Park, NY: Thompson Delmar Learning.

- Skinner, R.A., & Piek, J.P. (1994). Psycho-social implications of poor motor coordination in children and adolescents. In P.J. Beek & P.C.W. van Wieringen (Eds.), *Human Movement Science, 20,* 73-94.

- Skinner. R.A., & Piek, J.P. (2001). Psycho-social implications of poor motor coordination in children and adolescents. In P.J. Beek & P.C.W. van Wieringen (Eds.), *Human Movement Science, 20,* 73-94.

- Skorji, V., & McKenzie, B. (1997). How do children who are clumsy remember modelled movements? *Developmental Medicine and Child Neurology, 39,* 404-408.

- Smith Myles, B., & Simpson, R.L. (2001). Understanding the hidden curriculum: An essential social skill for children and youth with Asperger syndrome. *Intervention in School and Clinic, 36*(5), 279-286.

- Smits-Engelsman, B.C.M., Henderson, S.E., & Michels, C.G.J. (1998). The assessment of children with developmental coordination disorders in the Netherlands: The relationship between the Movement Assessment Battery for Children and the Korperkoordinations Test fur Kinder. In A.L. Barnett, L. Kooistra, & S.E. Henderson (Eds.), *Clumsiness as syndrome and symptom.* In H.T.A. Whiting & M.G. Whiting (Eds.), *Human Movement Science, 17*(4-5), 699-709.

- Smits-Engelsman, B.C.M., Niemeijer, A.S., & van Galen, G.P. (2001). Fine motor deficiencies in children diagnosed as DCD based on poor grapho-motor ability. In P.J. Beek & P.C.W. van Wieringen (Eds.), *Human Movement Science, 20*(1-2), 161-182.

- Smyth, M.M., & Anderson, H.I. (1999, October). *Coping with clumsiness in the school ground: Social and physical play in children with coordination impairments.* Paper presented at the 4th Biennial workshop on children with Developmental Coordination Disorder: From Research to Diagnostics and Intervention. Groningen, The Netherlands.

- Smyth, M.M., & Mason, U.C. (1998). Direction of response in aiming to visual and proprioceptive targets in children with and without developmental coordination disorder. In A.L. Barnett, L. Kooistra, & S.E. Henderson (Eds.), *Clumsiness as syndrome and symptom.* In H.T.A. Whiting & M.G. Whiting (Eds.), *Human Movement Science, 17*(4-5), 515-539.

- Smyth, T.R., & Glencross, D. (1986). Information processing deficits in clumsy children. *Australian Journal of Psychology, 38,* 13-22.

References

- Sprinkle, J., & Hammond, J. (1997). Family, health, and developmental background of children with developmental coordination disorder. *Australian Educational and Developmental Psychologist, 14*(1), 55-62.

- Stott, D.H., Moyes, F.A., & Henderson, S.E. (1972). *Test of motor impairment.* Guelph, ON, Canada: Brook Educational.

- Sugden, D.A., & Keogh, J.F. (1990). Problems in movement skill development. In H.G. Williams (Ed.), *Growth, motor development, and physical activity across the lifespan.* Columbia, SC: University of South Carolina Press.

- Symes, K. (1972). Clumsiness and the sociometric status of intellectually gifted boys. *Bulletin of Physical Education, 9,* 35-40.

- Thomas, J.R. (1984). *Motor development through childhood and adolescence.* Minneapolis, MN: Burgess Publishing Company.

- Thompson, S. (1997). *The source for nonverbal learning disorders.* East Moline, IL: LinguiSystems, Inc.

- Thompson, S. (2000). Nonverbal learning disabilities. *NLD on the Web.* *http://www.nldontheweb.org/thompson-1.htm*

- Thompson, S. (2000). Nonverbal learning disorders revisited in 1997. *http://www.nldontheweb.org/thompson-2.htm*

- Trott, M.C., Laurel, M.K., & Windeck, S.L. (1993). *SenseAbilities: Sensory integration.* Tucson, AZ: Therapy Skill Builders.

- Tsatsanis, K.D. (2005, April). Diagnostic boundaries and clinical characteristics: Autism, Asperger syndrome, and NLD. *Non-Verbal Learning Disabilities Conference.* Calgary, AB, Canada: The University of Calgary.

- van Dellen, T., & Geuze, R.H. (1988). Motor response programming in clumsy children. *Journal of Child Psychology and Psychiatry, 29,* 489-500.

- van Dellen, T., Vaessen, W., & Schoemaker, M (1990). Clumsiness: Definition and selection of subjects. In A.F. Kalverboer (Ed.), *Developmental biopsychology* (pp. 150-152). Ann Arbor, MI: University of Michigan Press.

References

• Visser, J.R.H., Geuze, R.H., & Kalverboer, A.F. (1998). The relationship between physical growth, the activity level and the development of motor skills in adolescence: Difference between children with DCD and controls. In A.L. Barnett, L. Kooistra & S.E. Henderson (Eds.), *Clumsiness as syndrome and symptom.* In H.T.A. Whiting & M.G. Whiting (Eds.), *Human Movement Science, 17*(4-5), 573-608.

• Volman, M.J.M., & Geuze, R.H. (1998). *Relative phase stability of bimanual and visuomanual rhythmic coordination patterns in children with a developmental coordination disorder.* In A.L. Barnett, L. Kooistra, & S.E. Henderson (Eds.), *Clumsiness as syndrome and symptom.* In H.T.A. Whiting & M.G. Whiting (Eds.), *Human Movement Science, 17*(4-5), 541- 572.

• Vygotsky, L.S. (1956). Learning and mental development at school age. In A.N. Leontiev & A.R. Luria (Eds.), *Selected psychological works* (written in 1938). Chapter provided in EDPS 693.14. Calgary, AB, Canada: The University of Calgary.

• Vygotsky, L.S. (1978). *Mind in society: The development of higher order psychological processes* (M. Cole, V. John-Steiner, S. Scribner, & E. Souberman, Eds. & Trans.) (Original works published 1930-1935). Cambridge, MA: Harvard University Press.

• Waldo, S.L., McIntosh, D.E., & Koller, J.R. (1999). Personality profiles of adults with verbal and nonverbal learning disabilities. *Journal of Psychoeducational Assessment, 17*(3), 196-206.

• Wall, A.E. (1982). Physically awkward children: A motor development perspective. In J.P. Das, R.F. Mulcahy, & A.E. Wall (Eds.), *Theory and research in learning disabilities* (pp. 253-268). New York: Plenum Press.

• Wall, A.E., Reid, G., & Paton, J. (1990). The syndrome of physical awkwardness. In G. Reid (Ed.), *Problems in movement control* (pp. 283-316). Amsterdam, The Netherlands: Reed Elsevier.

• Walton, J.N., Ellis, E., & Court, S.D.M. (1962). Clumsy children: Developmental apraxia and agnosia. *Brain, 85,* 603-612.

- Wann, J.P., Mon-Williams, M., & Rushton, K. (1998). Postural control and coordination disorders: The swinging room revisited. In A.L. Barnett, L. Kooistra & S.E. Henderson (Eds.), *Clumsiness as syndrome and symptom*. In H.T.A. Whiting & M.G. Whiting (Eds.), *Human Movement Science, 17*(4-5), 491-513.

- Watkins, M.W. (1999). Diagnostic utility of WISC-III subtest variability among students with learning disabilities. *Canadian Journal of School Psychology, 15*(1), 11-20.

- Wechsler, D. (1991). *Wechsler intelligence scale for children (3rd ed.)*. San Antonio, TX: The Psychological Corporation.

- Wechsler, D. (2003). *Wechsler intelligence scale for children (4th ed.)*. San Antonio, TX: The Psychological Corporation.

- Weingarten, G. (1980). The contribution of athletic and physical variables to social status in Israeli boys. *International Journal of Physical Education, 17,* 23-26.

- Wessel, J.A. (1976). *I CAN fundamental skills*. Austin, TX: PRO-ED.

- Whiting, H.T.A., & Whiting, M.G. (Eds.) (1998). *Human Movement Science, 17*(4-5).

- Wickstrom, R.L. (1983). *Fundamental motor patterns (3rd ed.)*. Philadelphia, PA: Lea & Febiger.

- Wigglesworth, R. (1963). The importance of recognising minimal cerebral dysfunction in pediatric practice. In M. Bax & R. MacKeith (Eds.), Minimal cerebral dysfunction. *Little Club Clinics in Developmental Medicine, 10,* 34-38.

- Wilbarger, P., & Wilbarger, J.L. (1991) *Sensory defensiveness in children aged 2-12: An intervention guide for parents and other caretakers*. Santa Barbara, CA: Avanti Educational Programs.

- Williams, H.G. (2002). Motor control in children with developmental coordination disorder. In S.A. Cermak & D. Larkin (Eds.), *Developmental coordination disorder* (pp. 117-13). Clifton Park, NY: Thompson Delmar Learning.

References

References

- Williams, H.G., Woolacott, M.H., & Ivry, R. (1992). Timing and motor control in clumsy children. *Journal of Motor Behavior, 24,* 165-172.

- Williams, K. (2001). Understanding the student with Asperger syndrome: Guidelines for teachers. *Intervention in School and Clinic, 36*(5), 259-265.

- Wilson, P., & McKenzie, B.E. (1998). Information processing deficits associated with developmental coordination disorder: A meta-analysis of research findings. *Journal of Child Psychology and Psychiatry, 39,* 829-840.

- Wilson, P.H., Maruff, P., Ives, S., & Currie, J. (2001). Abnormalities of motor praxis imagery in children with DCD. In P. J. Beek & P.C.W. van Wieringen (Eds.), *Human Movement Science, 20*(1-2), 135-159.

- Winders, P.C. (1997). *Gross motor skills in children with Down syndrome: A guide for parents and professionals.* Bethesda, MD: Woodbine House, Inc.

- Wing, L. (1981). Asperger's syndrome: A clinical account. *Psychological Medicine, 11*(1), 115-129.

- Wing, L. (1998). The history of Asperger's syndrome. In E. Schopler, G. Meisbov, & L.J. Kunce (Eds.), *Asperger's Syndrome or High Functioning autism?* (pp. 11-28).

- Winzer, M. (1990). *Children with exceptionalities: A Canadian perspective (2nd ed.).* Scarborough, ON, Canada: Prentice-Hall Canada, Inc.

- World Health Organization (1996). *International classification of diseases (ICD): Multi-axial classification of child and adolescent psychiatric disorders (10th ed.).* Cambridge, UK: Cambridge University Press.

- Wright, H.C., Sugden, D.A., Ng, R., & Tan, J. (1994). Identification of children with movement problems in Singapore: Usefulness of the Movement ABC checklist. In S.E. Henderson, S.E. (Ed.), *Developmental coordination disorder.* In G. Reid (Ed.), *Adapted Physical Activity Quarterly, 11*(2), 150-157.

- Yack, E., Sutton, S., & Aquilla, P. (1998). *Building bridges through sensory integration.* Weston, ON, Canada: Print 3.

26-05-987654321